Also by Don Mitchell

THUMB TRIPPING
FOUR-STROKE

The Souls of Lambs

THE SOULS OF LAMBS

A Fable

TEXT BY DON MITCHELL

DRAWINGS BY GEORGANN SCHROEDER

HOUGHTON MIFFLIN COMPANY
BOSTON 1979

Library of Congress Cataloging in Publication Data
Mitchell, Donald Earl.
    The souls of lambs.

    I. Schroeder, Georgann.   II. Title.
PZ4.M6796So   [PS3563.I75]   813'.5'4   78–25835
ISBN 0–395–27572–5

Printed in the United States of America
M 10 9 8 7 6 5 4 3 2 1

To Ethan

❧ Contents

The Souls of Lambs

1 ❧ *The Conception of the Lamb*

THERE IS EVIL IN THIS WORLD, AND GOOD, AND BOTH ARE necessary to life. So a lamb, a little thing, but living, needs to have a soul.

Before the lamb was born he was conceived. Before he was conceived — in a moment, in a ewe — he did not exist. *Something* existed. Seed; but there is no soul in seed. Eggs; but there is no soul in ova.

As for seed, the ram had many. Millions. For he had not tupped in very nearly one whole year. Sheep are not like men, they will not tup except a ewe be fertile, and fertility is timed to match the seasons of the year. Fertility begins when summer ends.

It begins in August.

The shepherd had feared the heat of August. Seed cannot tolerate hot weather. So the shepherd took his ram aside and held him close and sheared his belly wool, and particularly he clipped the ram's cod of its wiry wool. For wool is warm, and it is in these horse-eye testicles that seed is stored.

The shepherd feared the heat of August, but at the same time he employed it. He made hay. He had also hayed in June; but he wanted this second cut for winter, knowing that the as-yet-unborn and unconceived lamb would hunger one day for green grass, but on that day the pastures would lie frozen under snow. A second cut: Because the first is stemmy and unpalatable to a lamb, but a second cut is tender leaves and flowers caught at midbloom, caught suspended in their own cycle of setting seed, of making preparations against winter.

For years the shepherd had hayed with his son and his two daughters. Growing winter feed for several hundred sheep meant family work. In those days he might mow twenty acres in a single day, confident of willing hands to help him put a thousand bales in the barn ahead of rain. But his daughters became wives, in time, and his son moved south to work in some tall office building. The shepherd sold some of his land, reduced his flock and learned to hay alone. This was slower — riskier — and good weather meant everything.

All the art of making hay lies in prognosticating weather. Apart from this, the shepherd's work was simply to run old machines beneath the baking sun. Even lifelong haymakers can fail, though, in predicting weather — for nature, who is all our mother, is not easily predicted. Fair skies make grass into hay; storms can rot it to brown mulch. Forecasting is everything. The perfect forecast, which the shepherd's very bones learned to report, was the prospect of three fine fair cloudless days, three in a row. It happened every summer, once or twice, and sometimes more often; but the three days had to be foreseen quite early the first morning.

For many years before he hayed this second cut to feed yet unborn, unconceived lambs in winter, the shepherd had studied weather. Not in books, although he might have, but a book presents a thing like weather in a neat and codified manner, and this is not enough for haying. The shepherd had lived — patient, watching, like a lifelong student — and though he had not attained a perfect knowledge, though he could not, yet he had got the feel of weather well enough to sight ahead, to hazard a prognostication, to rise and to squint into a dawning sun and feel it coming: haying weather: three fine fair hot cloudless days. Three in a row.

More than once he had been wrong, though. Sometimes it had cost a hay crop. Once it had cost much more.

The shepherd hitched the mower to his tractor. Steel teeth gleamed along the sickle bar, sharp unto destruction, for their business was the death of grass. The shepherd remembered, then, what he never could forget, what had perverted and undone and deeply changed his life. And made him a philosopher. He had hayed the day his wife died.

Before he mowed his fields, the shepherd sought out his thirty sheep on pasture where they grazed and fattened, and he took his ram aside. Because the haying weather — these hot days to make grass into tender hay to feed unborn, unconceived and yet expected lambs in winter — this same heat would kill the seed which has no soul and yet without which no soul can begin to be: for no lamb would live to bear it. The shepherd took his ram aside, and penned him in a corner of the barn away from sun and cooled by shade and also by such breezes as would blow between the barn's rough boards. The shepherd drew water for his ram, to quench a thirst of hot summer days. And the shepherd fed his ram green hay — not leafy second-cut hay that a lamb would relish, but fit nourishment for rams. And then the shepherd mowed his fields.

All that first day the sun beat as he cut the green grass: killed it: millions upon millions of leaves and stems and flowers wilting where they fell helter-skelter in the mower's swath. And the grasses gave their moisture back to the air, which one day would give it back to the soil, where pale roots would lick it up to grow green blades of grass again.

On the second day the shepherd hitched the tractor to the rake, a graceful and a quiet machine devised of wheels and reels and fingers: steel wheels trailing the old tractor through the meadow, wheels driving reels lined with fingers all attached by springs. Driving this device, the shepherd picked up the millions of leaves and stems and flowers of the wilting drying grass, and tossed each in the air and tumbled each along the canted length of the clicking rake, building up behind him fluffy windrows where again the water in the grass could return to the air — but slowly now, the blades shading each other from the sun's harsh heat. While these blades were drying, dead, even then new life began to burst forth in their cells: Flora too small for the eye to see were living tiny lives, fermenting sugars in the grass. Life in death; and, for their work, the hay would be very palatable for a lamb in February.

The shepherd remembered: Haying, he had lost his wife.

The third day, these tiny creatures also died — of desiccation. Dried, whole grassy windrows could be raked together easily, high and wide now, waiting for the baler's noisy chomping mouth.

Sun-dried grass — hay — once made, must be kept from sun and rain. Too much sun would bleach it yellow white and leach the good away. Rain or dew would foster more ferment than is beneficial, till hay molds and rots and becomes unpalatable to a lamb. And unpalatable to a barn — for all creatures make heat, and the flora that live in wet hay may throw such heat that they start a fire. Many barns have thus been leveled.

The shepherd was relieved when nature, who is all our mother, dealt with him as he had hoped and as he had prognosticated. Late on the third afternoon he walked his windrows, teasing them with a pitchfork. He saw that his grass was dry: was new-made hay.

He hitched his baling machine to the tractor, and paraded the contraption up and down the windrows. The machine ground steel teeth and spun its tireless auger and consumed the hay: chopping it neat, packing it tight, tying it snug with lengths of twine. The shepherd remembered, then, the afternoon he lost his wife. He was driving this same machine across these very fields, while she died. In childbirth.

It had been three years ago. Though she was well over forty, though the children she bore in her youth were now all grown, were adults, still when she discovered her womb ripening again with child she never considered but that she would nurse another infant. That had been a hot and

Teasing windrows

an uncomfortable pregnancy. Time had made the woman frail. The shepherd himself had doubts about being a father again; for he too had lost youth's strength.

On the day she would have been delivered, he was baling hay — and baling feverishly, because the weather had betrayed him. Thunderheads loomed high by noon, and he plainly smelled a storm. Breaking off for lunch, his wife said gently that she was in labor. Early labor — and her labors of twenty-odd years ago had all been lengthy. She had passed a little blood; she recognized the low backache — her eyes shone as she informed him. He asked, should they start now? For the hospital was thirty miles away. Finish baling, she had urged him. Else the hay crop would be lost.

He did not need much convincing. He knew what his hay was worth — what purchased hay could cost. So he baled. But by three o'clock the storm clouds burst and drenched his bales where they lay scattered across the mown fields. Haying by himself, he had not allowed time to load his wagons.

All was not lost — if the storm passed quickly, if the sun emerged. But further work was useless. Instead, he would take his wife across the county to give birth. He entered his house and called her; she made no reply. He shouted. When he found her she lay still, and her ruptured womb no longer urged an infant to be born.

Today, not one cloud marred the sky. The baler did its work; the sun set. In the gloaming the shepherd threw neat square bales on his wagon and drove them to the barn and stacked them where, in six months, he would break them open to feed lambs.

Before the lamb was born he was conceived. Before he was conceived — in a moment, in a ewe — he did not exist. Something yet existed: ewe and ram, each with its own soul. And between them there existed an ancient chemistry, an instinct, an attraction unbridled, unbridlable, not at all times but according to the seasons on the earth, according to the sun circling in season. I speak of the lengths of days.

All through spring, as days grow longer, brighter, warmer, spirits lift in sheep and men alike. In midsummer, green pastures are bathed in light for two of each three hours in the day. In such warmth, in spring's rebirth and summer's bright abundance, hardly any ewe might feel the longing in her loins that says: Our lives are not all summers. There is evil in this world, and good. Contentment and privation. Warmth and chilling to the bone. And how may a man or creature stand up to the facts of winter? How may one endure a world growing daily hostile to us, till it would dispatch our lives except we made long preparations? Not because our mother, who is nature, bears ill will toward us — nor toward any living thing. She is: We owe her life and breath, but she weans quite perfectly. What sustains us through our winters is not nature's mothering but patterns of deliberate caring for ourselves and others. Husbandries: the care of households.

In August ewes perceive the days are growing shorter. As how could they not perceive it, grazing every day outdoors? And as ewes admit the prospect of short days, and longer nights, and cold winter sweeping inexorably across the earth — I say ewes admit this not as persons might, but in their souls — this prospect of cold brings forth a heat within, internal heat, much as wilting, dying grass creates a heat of fermentation. What is this heat? It is the longing for a lamb, the longing to confront the threat of winter with new life, a new creation, moist and poking at the breast, defiant of cold and snow. And to have this lamb, to be delivered of this creature with a soul in time to lift the spirit in the dead of winter — to accomplish this, a ewe must come in heat in early August, while the sun still beats down hot, while summer just starts to wane.

The shepherd wondered how the heat must feel. He knew that the heat of ewes is not like the heat of the mare, or the bitch; nor like the heat of the cow, or the cat; nor like the nanny goat's heat. The heat of ewes is a more quiet thing, without a bray or whine or rearing kick or any show of stamping. Ewes in heat stand still. Their eyes moon up, and they look self-possessed.

Is it like the tides? the shepherd wondered. A great rolling inside, a deep rumbling warmth within? On an August eve, in moonlight, he stood regarding his white ewes on pasture, feeling with them the ebb of light, the end of summer days. And he thought: A woman's cycle is too nearly like that of the moon for hazard to account for. A matter of some twenty-nine days, twelve hours, forty-four minutes, two and one-half seconds — who would dare to say there is no correlation? And he thought: A ewe's cycle is quite nearly half that of a woman's. One day's heat, then fourteen days to cycle the heat round again. The shepherd could not understand this heat. But he thought: A very tide, a great rolling warmth within, a deep longing tuned to sun and moon to nurse a lamb in winter.

The shepherd could not understand this heat. But he had felt a different fire in his loins time and again, a fire to race his pulse and make him stand up in a strength that, strangely, quivered like no strength at all: like a very weakness. Such a fire seemed to him the strongest force a man could know. Stronger than grief; and he knew of grieving. Strong like birth and death. Strong as motherhood is to a woman. Strong; but he thought there was a greater force on earth. That force was husbandry, which ram or ewe could never understand. Husbandry was greater; but it had great weaknesses.

The shepherd went to his barn and held his ram and lifted him and told him these things, though sheep cannot understand the language or the thoughts of people. While he spoke, the shepherd trimmed the ram's hoofs with a sharpened blade, so the ram could run nimbly with the flock and tup each ewe. And the shepherd made his ram a gift of corn, to give him vigor. The ram ate with fire in his eyes, and stamped the bedded barn floor, and he lowered his head and hurtled his two hundred pounds hard through the air to butt his skull against the shepherd's legs — this in thanks for corn. The shepherd buckled in his knees to receive the blow; and this battering well pleased him. In a creature ruled utterly by so powerful a force as fire to tup — I say desire; I say passion — in such a creature vigor is becoming. In such a creature vigor is a beautiful adornment.

The next day the shepherd turned his ram in with the ewes on pasture, so that he could run and chase and tup them every one in turn. The shepherd watched him chase them as a flock, racing up and down the field in the happy frenzy of boys chasing girls about a schoolyard. With this difference: Schoolboys choose girls with their eyes, but this ram chose with his nostrils. For there is a universe of scenting unbeknown to men who stand and walk on two hind legs and lift their faces from the earth. The other world, theirs, may be richer; may be vastly richer. Sights there are that drive men mad with lust, but how much more maddening to be a ram and smell the heat of ewes.

While the shepherd watched, a ewe chose not to run so fast against the ram's pursuit. She slowed, then she halted altogether. And the shepherd watched the black nostrils of his black-faced ram flare out and tremble in an act of scenting, an olfaction so intense it rippled and distorted all his face. Muscles tightened cracking wide his mouth and baring upper gums, and all the skin upon his head was wrinkled as a plain in earthquake. He poised this face above the ewe's hind flank, and she turned her head partway round to look just once, to look the hyena of desire just once in the eye.

The shepherd thought: So little of our lives is heat and passion; without husbandry love counts for nothing, heat cannot endure, and yet husbandries would have no purpose were it not for those few times in our passing lives when our hearts explode in conflagration. And the ram reared up, and threw his brisket on the ewe's firm back, and dug his forelegs in her ribs just where her broad hips began; and in a matter of quick seconds he had rammed an aching stylus deep inside her, thrusting past her vulva, deep inside, giving her his seed. And though in seed there is no soul, yet without seed there is not the possibility of soul.

The hyena of desire

The ewe stood still, receptive.

After coitus, all the beasts are sad. The shepherd well remembered. For this union is a ghost of Union, and it passes quickly. No one runs to see a fire quenched; we run to see the burning. The ewe turned round again to eye the ram, no longer frenzied. The shepherd regarded the ewe's face, the ewe in whom fresh seed were racing now toward a destination that no sheep could comprehend. Yet the shepherd saw a woman's eyes on the white ewe's face. He had seen these eyes too often, and still not enough: eyes that said, We have succumbed, we two, to fire and to passion, to creatureliness. Yet now I may have responsibilities. Will you? What if in my flesh new flesh and a new soul must be formed? What if in short months I have to squeeze a baby through my loins, in pain and in love? Will you care? What if your love and pain were of a moment now long passed? Can we two whose fires were as one for that one moment, can our fates be now so different? How can you —

The shepherd watched his black-faced ram back off two paces, drop his head and charge the ewe with all his strength. He sent her sprawling on lush grass.

The sheep's heat lasts some thirty hours. In that time the ewe and ram graze side by side, off from the others, and they tup every few minutes if a man would care to count. The ram is a creature of olfaction, and the ewe throws from her parts such a maddening scent he cannot leave her

Sprawling on lush grass

side. For all the world they look married in that day. But toward the end of heat, her body undertakes a different project, and a cooler one: an ovulation. A princess floats down the winding staircase to receive the suitors swimming toward her. The shepherd thought: I mistrust yet I need anthropomorphisms. I must have them, or I cannot ever understand. And I would understand these mysteries, how it is that even for a lamb the world's a place of good and evil, warmth and certain chilling, necessary goods and necessary evils, so that even a lamb — such a little thing, but living — even a lamb must needs have a soul.

Of all the creatures that men breed for meat to nourish themselves, the proportions of a sheep are most like those of humankind. A fit ewe at tupping weighs some hundred and twenty pounds. A ram weighs, say, sixty more. A lamb is born weighing between five and eleven pounds — and most often eight, like a human baby. The womb and the vagina of a ewe have very nearly the proportions of a woman's womb and a woman's vagina; of these facts, barnyard humorists have joked for centuries. So the scale of the stage on which a lamb is made, on which a soul is now created — the scale of this stage is known to every human being. This is not the cavern of a cow, nor the groove of field mice, nor the declivity of rabbits. This is space like our own, space that we can comprehend. Who has not considered its dimensions? We can comprehend this. What cannot be comprehended is what happens on that stage.

Heat is passed, but conception is not yet completed. An army of seed, each without soul and yet each bearing the possibility of soul, an anarchic army all in broken ranks now charges headlong toward an egg. The egg looms vastly larger than seed and yet it is tiny — tiny as lambs or most living creatures go. And neither is there soul in egg, but like seed every egg contains the possibility of soul. There is no comprehending this, any more than one can comprehend life itself. How a seed — and just one — how a seed, which is material, can find and penetrate an egg, itself material, and how after that no other seed may enter, for a soul is born — no, not born but created; no, not created but conceived — there can be no comprehending, for this soul is immaterial. It is a miracle. All his life a man could search and never spy the living soul; yet without this soul a lamb is only flesh, only meat.

The shepherd had not seen the soul depart his wife. What he saw was only flesh. So: She had been well past early labor. She might have been mistaken. Or perhaps it came on quickly. He knew wombs could rupture with scant warning, scant external bleeding. He had seen it in old sheep. His wife too was past the age for childbearing. He could see her now weighing her pain, and urging him to bale. Better lose a hay crop than his mate, though — and a helpless infant. Then rain fell in sheets and he knew that his hay would also rot.

How does anyone confront such evil? How do men bear grief? The shepherd had crumpled on the bed and clutched hands at his heart, astonished by its violent beating. He feared it might burst. He feared death — no, not death, but the dying. Death itself was easy — death was manifested here, death was being simply meat. An issue of blood. Pain shot toward the shepherd's shoulder. But he saw succumbing now would be a cruel, pointless joke. He vowed: No, I will not die today. I still am more than meat.

The shepherd did not weep. His heart regained its ancient pace. Slowly, then, he rose and sought help.

How does anyone confront such evil? How do men bear grief? How indeed, had we not our souls to teach us to endure. Things there are on earth which can't be seen, not with the naked eye, not with microscopes or binoculars or any lens. Things there are within each creature which can never be explained. To wit: What is the soul, and where? And yet the soul does certainly exist while creatures live; there is no life without soul; and when creatures die it is their souls that die, or disappear, for not even a single cell of carcass disappears — yet something has been lost, or changed.

The shepherd watched a lamb conceived, and thought: I know three ways to see the soul, though not with eyes. Each is a mode of loving, each a mode of loving vision. One mode is passion. And a second mode is motherhood. And a third way to see the soul is in husbandry.

2 ❧ The Lamb Grows Within a Ewe

FOR TWENTY-ONE WEEKS THE CONCEIVED BUT UNBORN lamb lived in a warm, dark, moist, rumbling cave. A womb. He did not know that he lived there; he had never been outside. He had never seen the wide world, though within days of conception he possessed what would become his eyes. Nor had he tasted food, though he had a mouth. Nor gamboled across grassy fields, though he had four slender legs each tipped by a two-toed hoof.

The work of a lamb lying living in a womb is growth: is preparation to endure the world of sheep and men. So the lamb grew within a ewe. The soul of the lamb, however, never grew. It simply was.

There is evil in this world, and good, and both are necessary. For a lamb to grow is good. But the lives of creatures go on only by expending life: by killing, by incorporation of the dead into the living. Lying in a dark womb, the little lamb was not yet killing. Yet he was involved in killing, he was a beneficiary of killing. A ewe and mother did his killing for him, and fed him every day as much as he desired, so that one day he could graze and eat — and kill — on his own.

The shepherd had not at first considered his sheep killers. They did not kill grass completely, but only grazed on it. Grazed, the grasses could not flower and set seed as they desired, yet they did not die and they could even reproduce themselves another way, by sending runners out across the ground. Sheep *can* kill grass, by overgrazing; but that is the fault of careless shepherds, not of sheep. Because husbandry is all about fences, about putting enough sheep on pastures and yet not too many, that sheep and grass alike may prosper.

The shepherd had not at first considered his sheep to be killers, though they certainly frustrated grasses trying to set seed. He considered them gentle gourmets of the salad. The shepherd himself loved greens, and loved to chew on crisp, moist lettuce. Pasture, though, would be an endless salad. Would he tire of that? Perhaps. Yet he thought: *Dozens* of different greens grew in his pastures. What if each grass had its unique taste, and each weed? — for sheep eat weeds, and brush, too, and even leaves that fall from trees.

The shepherd thought: These grazing ewes may well be epicures. Why else do they shuffle — patient, searching — up and down the pasture, if not to compose fine gustatory harmonies? How many ways, the shepherd wondered, might timothy taste? The creased leaves might be quite different from the stems. And what of the plant's state of bloom, whether tender juicy shoots or with the fuzz just heading up or in full bloom, all covered with the dusky blue of pollen? And what of combining in one mouthful timothy and clover? Or trefoil, or the broad-leaved brome, or waving lespedeza? The shepherd thought: Sheep must be gastronomes. And perhaps I would not tire of pasture, if I could digest it.

The shepherd had not at first considered his sheep killers. In fact, he had started breeding sheep out of admiration for their pacific digestion: green grass in, dark pellets out, and daily gains of flesh and wool. From new grass at Easter till the first hard winter snows, sheep could harvest every meal themselves. And spread their dung unaided, working it into the soil to nourish grass again. No plow would ever have to bite the pasture sod and turn it, no harrows would rip apart the warp and woof of roots of grasses holding earth in place against the wind and rain and baking sun. Yet the grass upon the land would grow a food to nourish men: Grass would grow the flesh of lambs. And wool to warm men in cold winter. And all because these creatures hide four stomachs in their bellies.

The ewe carrying a lamb within her loins eats grass. She swallows grass into a vat, a paunch, a rumen: a dark hall of fermentation. As mown hay ferments in drying, bringing forth a heat within to match the heat of summer sun, so in the rumen dying blades of grass support new life. We speak here of flora: of bacteria: of microscopic creatures more ancient than sheep or men. We speak here of tiny creatures by the billions, by the trillions, each an organism of decay. Ewes eat grass, and in this they kill few plants. But the ewe can digest blades of grass no better than can men. *Bacteria* digest grass. Then the ewe digests bacteria.

Peace: a ewe heavy in lamb

The ewe cannot know this. But she pokes from one plant to another, biting clean the blades that long to rise and flower and set seed. Swallowing these greens, she sets a daily table for the hordes that feed within her. And she serves them carefully, upon peril of her life: for the flora that eat timothy are not those that eat brome, and neither could digest a sudden glut of lush alfalfa — or of any new food, unless it be patiently introduced.

As a vat of fermentation bubbles and produces gas, so a rumen belches to the air. The ewe feeds her flora, and the flora feed the ewe. We speak here of killing, of rot and decay. The shepherd often thought no sight on earth was quite so peaceful as a ewe heavy in lamb sitting, legs tucked, chewing rhythmically on her grassy cud. But the peaceful ruminating sheep is not digesting grass; rather, she chews to help flora digest her grass for her. She is the white-robed brewer stirring up a frothy wort. Her contentment is that of a butcher, stropping steel blades; or of a shepherd, fattening winter lambs for Easter slaughter. When the work of flora is accomplished, when the fibrous grass is broken down to spring-green mush, then the organisms of decay are delivered wholesale to the ewe's true stomach — the fourth — where digestive juices greet them and dispatch their small lives: killing for a simple meal. Meat, homegrown and sacrificed.

The ewe cannot know this, not as men know. Not with words. Yet the soul of every living creature understands death: how death is a necessary evil, and a part of life. The soul understands this, and yet never has to brood upon it, not after the fashion of men when their thoughts grow morbid. The soul does not think. It is. And as the soul is life, so the soul accepts its necessary end. Even a lamb, a tiny thing, but living, growing, squirming, crouched in a dark womb, even a lamb has a living soul which knows of death.

The death of the shepherd's wife had made him brood; his thoughts grew morbid. Grief had ruled him for a season. This paradox angered him: He felt closer to his wife, dead, than he had for years in living. Sometimes he would let his heart race freely, urging its wild rhythms, as though to hasten the day he could lie again at her side in some cold and final Union.

For her death, he did not blame himself; or her. He knew that such things could happen. But they had been careless with themselves, as well as unlucky. Had they valued hay a little less, the woman might have lived. Or the infant, anyway — but he shuddered to think how he could have raised a child alone. That would have been worse luck. His wife had mothered expertly, and babies need good mothers.

Grief had turned his thoughts morbid, yet the shepherd's soul endured and never doubted what it knew. In time, he made a slow adjustment. Leave off farming, urged his children; and he had obliged them by visiting their new homes near cities. He did not stay long. Sheep were burdensome; yet he knew no other way to live. Finally he compromised and sold all but a dozen acres, purchasing then for himself a grand, eccentric luxury: the luxury of farming on an uneconomic scale. He sold ewes until he kept just thirty. He slowed his life down. And he vowed to do all things now with utter deliberation, with the patient care of one not old, but no longer young. He would never rush or be rushed, not ever again.

He began to think about the soul — the souls of men and lambs.

The lamb grows, although its soul does not. In the outside world, the world the lamb had never seen, seasons changed. First, the lush tupping pasture dried up in an August drought. Leaves of grass turned brown and shattered from their stems with a dead crackle as ewes browsed by, heading for the water trough. When the dry spell broke, cool autumn rains poured from the heavens as though nature, who is all our mother, had determined to create new rivers and seas. Where the feet of grazing ewes had trampled paths across the pasture, now dust turned to sticky mud. The white wool on each ewe's back was washed flat, slimming their figures, and their fleeces' yolky lanolin was scrubbed out by the rains.

The shepherd did not fear for his sheep's fleeces, though. He feared for their hoofs. So he led his ewe flock to the barn one day — in late September — and he penned them there and held them each in turn and trimmed their feet. For there are less beneficial flora in the world of sheep than those that digest grasses in a ewe's dark paunch. Others would digest whole hoofs. Particularly in the cool of autumn, when rains soak tired pastures, the shepherd had seen sheep lamed by a rotting so wild, so ferocious he had felt altogether helpless, and a failure as a husband.

Rot, he knew, was necessary. And it was both good and evil. Good and evil are both in this world by necessity, they are as two sides of one coin, we cannot have it otherwise. Digestion is rot. But without digestion, without eating, there can be no nourishment. And nourishment is good. Without passion — which is brief, and selfish, and consumes the heart — without passion how can creatures come to be conceived? Even motherlove, the greatest good on earth to an infant, even motherlove in time would cripple the young did they not wean themselves in anguish and desire for adulthood.

The shepherd knew he could not rid the world of rot — even those certain rots that threatened sheep. But his caring demanded he do what he could. So he dirtied himself trimming each ewe's feet, scraping down their hoofs so that no dung could cling and harbor rot, so those flora that would lame his sheep could scarcely gain a toehold. This is husbandry: a greater love than passion or than motherhood — superior in character because it does not spring from instinct — though husbandry is not as strong a love as these two others. Husbandry is *chosen* love. Yet in this a shepherd can see, if he would, the souls of lambs.

While the shepherd held each ewe, he made sure each had two sound teats. And he pressed each ewe's firm loins — not because he hoped that at one month he might feel a lamb which barely could have filled a teaspoon. No; but he wanted the living growing unborn lamb to feel him. To think — though he knew the lamb within a womb could never think it — to think: Very well, I seem to have a shepherd in the world.

The rains and the cooler weather set the grass to growing again. Now the shepherd puzzled over where to let the ewe flock graze. Grass is good; but too much of the finest grass may not be good, particularly when a ewe is early in her term. A lamb spends twenty-one weeks growing in its mother, and at birth it weighs about eight pounds. Half that weight is put on in the final month of pregnancy. If a ewe dines too well early in her term, her body fattens.

Now fat is a good thing in its place, but fat can hinder one. Particularly if one has to squeeze a lamb through groaning loins out into the wide world. The shepherd had, some years, allowed his pregnant ewes to fatten and then suffered with them for it on cold nights in late December. He had seen a lamb's wide shoulders lock against the birth canal, head in the world but hips trapped within the loins of an exhausted ewe. Fat can be a good thing in its place, but fat can hinder one. So the shepherd led his ewe flock back where they had fed all summer, where the grass was short and stunted by their endless patient grazing. Here they would grow fit, not fat; here their bodies' muscles would stay taut and toned unto the lambing. The ewes complained at first, for in the tupping pasture just across the fence the grass grew lush. But husbandry is all a matter of fences, of trying to set boundaries round the good and evil in this world. The shepherd determined that his ewes would remain lean and healthy.

All at once, it seemed, the sun was setting at the dinner hour. Although maples blazed with autumn, though the days grew warm with second summer, which is Indian summer, yet each evening's chill and clear light promised winter's sure arrival. And in winter is destruction. Vegetables proved it first — those garden plants that live so puffed with water that a single frost will blacken leaves and topple them. On such mornings every single blade of grass is packed in ice; but grasses can endure much frost — they never did aspire to be as swollen and voluptuous as red tomatoes.

Ewes are not surprised by autumn, or by all this frost and freezing. They detect the changing of the seasons while it is still summer, and they respond in a heat that is the wish to nurse a lamb in winter. Yet on a late October morn when snow commenced to fall from a slate-gray sky, the shepherd woke to hear his ewes cry bitterly. He went to see them, bringing the green comfort of a bale of hay. For nature, who is all our mother, had buried the grasses beneath moisture, crystalline and white. The shepherd comforted his ewes, inside whose wombs he knew that lambs were growing. He promised that this snow would melt off quickly, bringing back the pasture for a time. And till the sun appeared he promised to bring hay down to them: not tender hay he'd made in August, fit for lambs, but the coarser June-cut hay for feeding the ewe flock in winter.

The sheep ate the shepherd's hay. In good time the sun appeared and melted the snow to clear water which ran across the pasture, soaking deep into the earth to nourish grass again.

October passed. With November each brown leaf fell from each tree, and raw winds now made the ewe flock think of their warm barn, of hay and corn, and of how each might pass the winter nursing up a lamb. The shepherd was not ready to lead them to the barnyard. Nevertheless he walked in their pastures and pondered what they had to eat, and he felt compassion for them because all the grass was short. So he opened wide the gate into the lusher tupping pasture, though this pasture too was showing the effects of cold and wind, which lays grass sideways on the ground like a ewe's wet fleece.

The ewes hushed their bleating and their longing for the barnyard, and they harvested the lodging grasses in the tupping pasture for another fortnight. The shepherd was not loath to see them fill their bellies now; they had been growing lambs inside their wombs for three months. And their lambs would no longer have fit into a teaspoon, or a tablespoon, or even a child's play shovel. Now the ewes had swollen loins and sagging bellies. And just while a two-pound lamb's demands for food are growing urgent, so just then its size begins to displace room in a ewe's body. Now she breathes with difficulty ambling up a hill, and now she cannot fill her stomachs quite as full as when she had no lamb. The shepherd's wife had made the same complaint, heavy with child. So he was eager to see them graze the better of his pastures.

Now she breathes with difficulty

When deep snows first fell, it was Thanksgiving. And though grass might poke up once again, through melting drifts, the shepherd knew it was the end of that year's pasture season. In high boots he waded through the snow to find his ewes on pasture; seeing him they bleated and demanded winter barnyard comforts. The shepherd marveled that he had to shovel snow aside just to open gates to lead his ewes up to the barn. Summer is just long enough, he told them, for men to forget exactly what winter is like. But the ewes had not forgotten. They had been preparing since the sun first went into decline. And now they neared fruition.

Between Thanksgiving and Christmas a three-pound lamb crouched in a ewe becomes an eight-pound creature, large enough to make its own way in the world of sheep and men. For its mother, this is a hard time — as though she carried in her womb a huge demanding tapeworm. So the shepherd fed each ewe five pounds of hay each day, though three pounds would have served her own needs.

Five pounds of hay each day is nearly all a ewe can process — particularly with a lamb crowding her lungs and stomachs — yet five pounds of hay may not be quite sufficient for her needs. Especially if she bears twins. So the shepherd made his ewes a daily present of mixed corn and oats and wheat, half a pound to each. For, denied grain, he had witnessed ewes heavy in lamb turn sluggish, as if drugged, and lie upon the ground with sweet breath that augured death: the cloying poison which is acetone.

A ewe would give the growing lamb kicking in her womb everything he asks — more than she ought — and this is motherhood, a mystery and a force as strong in its way as is passion which consumes men's hearts. Motherhood and passion: There are no stronger forces than these, but there is a weaker, greater force and that is husbandry. Husbandry would treat the pregnant ewe or woman with great care. True, there were sheep in this world before there were shepherds; and they could not count on grain to eat when far gone in pregnancy. But neither did they live ten years and raise some twenty lambs; and the lambs they did raise were not often born weighing eight pounds, full of vigor and in strong flesh to face a northern winter. So the shepherd fed ewes grain: so that in their bodies' longing to nourish a lamb, they wouldn't fail to nourish their own selves and taste untimely death.

It was December, the darkest month, and the earth spun toward its fixed appointment with the solstice. Snows there were and bitter nights, and ewes huddling in the barn all bloated out with growing lambs. Starting with the week of Christmas, the shepherd rose each night between the hours of two and three, and dressed his body in wool clothes and pushed through snowdrifts to the barn. Ewes may drop their lambs at any time of day, yet they almost always choose the cold and dead of night.

The shepherd would sit with his ewes where they lay on straw, shining a lantern on each one in turn to watch her breathing. The souls of their lambs were yet unborn, locked tight in wombs. Yet the barn at that hour seemed fairly to overflow with the souls of lambs. And the shepherd would pick out which ewes were straining most to breathe, which winced as quick contractions gripped their loins — not acute contractions as in lambing's final throes, but short experimental tonings of the muscled womb.

The twenty-one weeks now were ending. The time was nigh. The living souls of living lambs were waiting to be born.

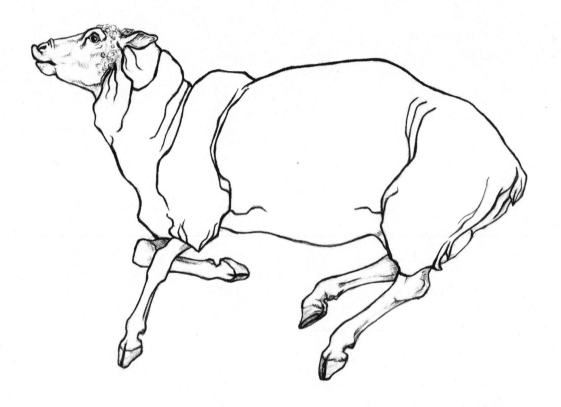

3 &⤳ The Birth of the Lamb

TWO DAYS AFTER CHRISTMAS, THE SHEPHERD ROSE IN THE night and dressed his body in wool clothes and walked through snowdrifts to the barn, as had become his custom. It was twelve degrees out, and quite dark, and snowing a fine powder that swirled round to hide his footprints as he left them.

In the barn he sat with his ewes on their bed of yellow straw, and he watched their breathing. There was one, a ewe he called Penelope, who held her breath and bared her upper gums and showed him round eyes wide with pain. Then she exhaled, sighing. The contraction passed; she filled her lungs again, watching the shepherd who watched her. The ewe stood. She pawed the bedstraw with a delicate white hoof. Her flanks hung sunken ahead of her hips, and then again she tightened the muscles all about her nose and mouth. The shepherd rubbed his hands to warm them, for the night was bitter, but his heart was glad because he knew by morning there would be a lamb to cheer the cold of winter.

The shepherd rose and held his ewe and spoke words to her softly. Not because he thought she understood, for sheep can never understand the language or the thoughts of humans. Not because he harbored the conceit that he could share the least iota of her pain, or of her triumph; these were hers and hers only. Not because he believed soft words from his human mouth could truly soothe her hard travail; he knew nothing about squeezing lambs from swollen muscled loins. Yet he spoke, and could not keep from speaking softly to his ewe: because he was her shepherd.

Again the shepherd sat, and turned his lantern off, and heard his ewe Penelope breathe in that still dark place. In a corner of the barn he had prepared a cot for this night — for all the nights of lambing — and covered it with old quilts and blankets. But now he was too alert to rest. The very barn had come alive with the souls of lambs.

The shepherd spoke softly to his straining ewe, and to her lamb. He said: To be born, that is the second hardest thing we creatures ever have to do. The second hardest in our lives, however short or long they be. Only dying is a harder task. Birth is a drawn-out pain, but for most its end is life and the world of the living. Do not mourn — he told his lamb, whom he had not even seen — do not mourn to leave the womb of your conception, never turn your head to look back as that home collapses on you.

The shepherd had delivered lambs into the world with their heads turned back to glimpse the womb, and these births had gone hard on ewe and lamb alike. He had pulled lambs tail-first from wombs while mothers screamed in pain. And some of those lambs had died of suffocation when their heads locked tight against the pelvic arch, and the umbilicus had broken. And he never could forget that other breech, that other lamb. Nature, who is all our mother, has no pity for those who would come into the wide world backward, gazing on the home they'd fled.

Penelope groaned in hard discomfort. She lay down, then stood; but there is no comfortable way to give birth to a lamb. The shepherd switched on his lantern, and he saw her flanks sink deep into her sides, and he watched her grind the wide molars far back in her mouth. When she turned he saw a glistening. Her vulva had gone soft, gone flabby, stretching even now to pass a lamb. No mistaking, this was labor; but it might be hours yet.

The shepherd's feet were cold. Were his wife alive, she would have sensed by now his absence from the bed and guessed a ewe was lambing. Then she might have risen and made tea and brought it out to share with him, and share the waiting. That woman's slender hands had entered many ewes to turn a backward lamb aright. She had better hands than his for that dark business. But he knew midwifery himself, where sheep were concerned, and he would not hesitate to thrust his arm in past the elbow to correct a breech.

Now the shepherd had no tea, and no wife to share this labor. Yet he reminded himself, while his wife lived they missed many lambings. With two hundred ewes all due inside a fortnight, they could not care for each. If just one lamb in ten were lost, they counted it a good year; and they comforted themselves thinking the lambs that died had been the weak ones. But lambs die of simple ills: cold; wandering off alone; failing to locate the teat. Simple care saves many lambs.

The shepherd took four wooden panels he'd made long ago, and nailed them together now to build a pen for ewe and newborn, apart from all the other sheep, so that they might come to know each other well. But he did not pen the ewe Penelope just yet. Some ewes, and some women, like to ease the pain of labor by walking about between contractions. So the shepherd held his ewe again, and urged her to walk if she needed, and he felt now underneath her for her warm, soft udder. And his heart was glad, because he knew a lamb loves milk.

The shepherd found his cot and brought it near the ewes that lay sleeping on the yellow straw. He drew the old quilts over his body, and closed his eyes. He did not fear sleeping through the lamb's birth. The ewe would wake him. A ewe far gone in labor makes a trumpeting so urgent and unsheeplike that it would astound the visitor. No shepherd can sleep through it. So the shepherd slept, and dreamed. He did not curse the cold of winter anymore, or its dark nights. His lambing season had begun.

The shepherd dreamed of birth. This is a tale of hope in dark December, a story of new life in the dead of winter. There is evil in this world, and good, and both are necessary, and they are as two sides of one coin. So life is squeezed forth in pain from the contracting womb. Pain for mother, pain for child. Let a creature live for eighty years, let it live a hundred but never will its body be gripped in that way again. As if to squeeze the very life from one, when all the while it is toward the world of life we travel. Woe to those who turn their heads and look back at the womb's collapsing!

The shepherd was wakened by rough gruntings in the dark. He switched on his lantern. Penelope had passed a water bag: a sac of amniotic fluid, which is all the ocean where a lamb swims while he grows within a ewe. The bag dangled from her parts, unbroken; but as he watched, the ewe pawed the ground and the sac swung in between her legs and caught upon her hocks and ruptured. The shepherd climbed in among his ewes, and he held Penelope to tell her it would not be long now.

The shepherd took his lantern to the shelves where he had laid out medicines and towels and ear tags and all he might need in lambing. He took down strong iodine to paint the lamb's umbilicus, because there are flora in this world that bode ill to lambs, that would enter a lamb's body through the unhealed navel. And he took a towel down from the shelf, because the night was cold and lambs are born soaked to the skin.

Crossing the dark barn, he passed the pen where his ram lay all alone and proud and unconcerned. Since bringing the flock in off pasture, the shepherd had had to pen his ram for fear his butting might cause a ewe to abort. The shepherd tried to tell his ram: Look, there, a ewe is lambing and you made that lamb with her, made it in a fit of heat and passion on an August morn. Now take pleasure in fruition. But the ram cared nothing for fruition, nor for little lambs. The shepherd left him snorting on his bed of yellow straw.

The shepherd sat down with Penelope to watch and wait. Between hard contractions she would bring up cud to chew, or nibble hay. She was not afraid to lamb. But when her loins contracted it was like a bellows in her belly, pumping her woolled flanks in spasms terrible to see. Perhaps the ram's attitude was the best that a man could take. The shepherd loved babies; but he well remembered feeling distant from his wife when, twenty-odd years ago, he had watched her labor. The muscle

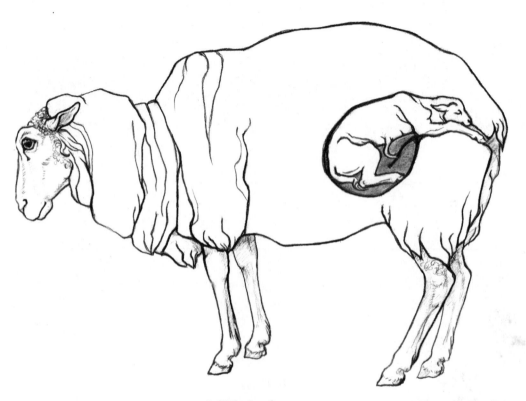

A little hoof emerges

in women — and in ewes — could disconcert a man. He had seen her legs lift off the bed and tremble violently. He had watched her stomach ripple. Had he been responsible for this? What men could not share, perhaps it made sense to view from a safe distance. Like his ram. But rams never struggle between passion and husbandry, never struggle in their hearts.

Penelope lay on her side, her legs stretched. She groaned. She strained to stand, then pawed the bedding as though to make a nest in all her pain. Her loins went stiff again and, from within the sac emerging from her sunken vulva, the shepherd watched a little hoof wave quickly at him. It disappeared. But with the next contraction it was back, and the shepherd smiled to see it poking from the ewe. Then another hoof appeared to join it, and these were front hoofs, two white clean aborning hoofs wrapped in pale mucous. Some few contractions later, he first saw the nose and mouth of a lamb's head presented facing forward on its knees.

This is the hardest part of squeezing a lamb from the loins. Nowhere is a lamb so wide as at the head and shoulders. Years ago, when he had more ewes than he could lamb out with care, the shepherd had liked to grasp the forelegs of a borning lamb and pull down when the ewe contracted, hastening its birth. That had been impatience, and poor husbandry. Now he was alone, and older, and he had no reason to rush or to be rushed; now he wanted only to do all things with deliberation. So he would not tamper with a mother's rhythm and her schedule. He knew it took time to stretch the rippling cervix wide, and haste might only tear the ewe inside and add to her discomfort.

The shepherd tucked his cold hands in his warmer armpits, and he was content to wait and watch the miracle again. The head emerged farther, far enough so that the lamb could open his small mouth and lick his lips with his tongue. The shepherd laughed. Already the borning lamb had it in mind to search for milk.

A little longer, and the head was clear. Yet the lamb refused to open his eyes, all awash in slime, half in the world, half out. The ewe Penelope took some few steps, nibbled hay and then fell on her side and flailed her limbs and pointed high her nose. The bellows of her flanks sunk in. She caught her breath and brought to bear her body's entire force. Thus the shoulders of the lamb were born.

Though a lamb's hindquarters slip easily from the womb, the shepherd was used to seeing mothers rest here, their hardest work accomplished. He had never used to let lambs dangle in midbirth. Now he rather liked to. It made birth more of a process, less an instant change of state. So, watching Penelope just collect her breath, he regarded the half-born's face.

Nothing in experience prepares a creature to be born — or to die. These are uncharted waters, filled with pains we dare not dwell on. It is meet that we forget our births, and spend the great bulk of our days in prevarication against the knowledge of our deaths; and yet we well know how to die, even as we once knew how to tolerate birth's pain. We know these things in our souls, which none of us has ever seen in quite the way we see most things. And yet when a ewe in heat turns to gaze on a ram's wild face, contorted with his passion — here two creatures see their souls, although not with the outer eye. And a shepherd in his tasks of husbandry, in daily caring, and particularly in the cold of a December lambing — here a man may see the soul, though not with the external eye.

With a final groan the ewe Penelope thrust out all the hindflanks of her lamb. It squirmed on yellow straw, and the ewe turned round to lick the birth slime from her lamb's wet nostrils, so that it could draw its first breath. And this is motherhood, another mode of vision of our souls, much like passion, much like husbandry, a means for living creatures to regard each other's souls, and their own — though not with the external eye.

The night was cold. The wispy ringlets of the lamb's fleece lay pasted to its back in birth slime, and also in yellow feces — meconium. Many creatures void in birth, and many will in dying. The ewe Penelope slapped her tongue to clean the lamb's face, and steam rose from its wet body. The lamb opened one eye, then the other. The lamb filled its lungs. The long umbilicus that joined it for twenty-one weeks to its mother had snapped now, a limp vestige. The lamb shook his head: as a diver might, surfacing from the deep. Or as one fighting off a long, engulfing sleep. For within its soul a lamb knows: the wide world begins here.

The shepherd feared to see the lamb's body shake and shiver. Yet he thought it better for Penelope to lick her lamb clean, while she had a mind to do so, than for him to wrap it in a towel. A ewe must learn her lamb's scent — which is at first her own scent, the scent of her womb — so that the bond of motherhood between them can be well established. The best thing a lamb can have in this world is a loving mother; no amount of care or feeding on a shepherd's part can fill the void an orphaned or a disowned lamb must face. So the shepherd let the newborn shiver some few minutes while his mother licked it clean.

While she licked, the lamb cried: a bleat at once uncertain yet insistent, quite in contrast to the grunts of labor that had lately filled the barn. And

Penelope licks her lamb clean

the ewe spoke to her lamb in a tender lowing murmur. And the shepherd thought: Why, I have heard this conversation, human lovers make it all atrembling in their passion. With my wife I spoke these words. This is soul to soul, here in the night barn. And he thought: I believe and I see that the soul exists, and that it teaches us to love the good and hate the evil that are in this world, and yet to accept them both, for both are necessary.

Finally the ewe nosed her lamb over, answering the only question left in the shepherd's mind: The lamb was not a ewe. And had not been a ewe, not ever, not from its moment of conception. Here lay a baby buck.

Sex is a creature's destiny, much more for sheep than humans. For a ram will never come in heat and grow a lamb within him; and a single ram can tup a flock of up to fifty ewes. To be born not a ewe is to face untimely death, death before the fruition that all living things aspire to. The shepherd would have been happier to see a ewe lamb — to increase some neighbor's flock, graze summer pastures and know heat; but he was not sad, because he knew the newborn creature would become fit meat for humans, for men's nourishment and health, as all living creatures must expend each other in good season. The shepherd was not sad, though a ewe would have made him happier; nor was he sorry for the kicking lamb. He was sorry only for its soul, to have to die untimely, even in the spring, before fruition. Yet he knew the soul knows how to die, even as it once knew how to endure birth's grip.

The shepherd rubbed the lamb in a warm towel, and he painted the umbilicus with strong iodine to keep infection out. And he considered whether this lamb had a twin or no. For this reason, above all, the

Four legs splayed on wobbly feet

shepherd tried to attend lambings: When a ewe has twins, she may forget the one and love the other in her fever and excitement, unless a shepherd compels her to accept them both. Before there were shepherds there were sheep, but they rarely twinned.

The shepherd held the lamb, and he considered that the lamb was large, and too heavy to have an unborn twin. Even then, Penelope's flanks shuddered in a hard contraction; but the shepherd guessed that she was straining to pass afterbirth — the red placenta from her womb — and not another lamb. The shepherd took the lamb and, holding it at the ewe's nose, he led both to the pen he had prepared for their first days together.

It was in this pen, some minutes later, that the lamb wobbled to his feet, his four legs splayed like flying buttresses to hold aloft his torso. Then one leg buckled, and he toppled sideways; but a moment later he was off the ground again. The shepherd laughed to see the miracle another time, for all a newborn lamb desires is milk, but he must discover milk and to do that he must stand and learn to walk and poke to find the breast.

The little lamb was eager to solve these problems. Within minutes he could take quick steps. He lunged his head at many parts of his mother's body which did not turn out to be breasts. Then he found the breast but missed the teat — or spat it out because he had not quite expected it, not just like that, not quite so soft and warm and pliant. The shepherd and the mother were content to wait, and yet the shepherd knew that in each teat had formed a waxy plug to keep first milk from leaking, and the lamb might grow quite hungry before sucking hard enough to clear these. So the shepherd held his ewe and stripped milk from each breast. And then he nudged the newborn lamb ahead to taste the miracle.

4 ❧ The Lamb Drinks Milk and Grows

THERE IS EVIL IN THIS WORLD, AND GOOD, AND BOTH ARE necessary, and both are as two sides of one coin. Yet some goods are so good as to be nearly unmitigated. Such is ewe's milk to a lamb.

The shepherd had seen hundreds of lambs squeezed into the wide world. Some came weak, some strong, some weighed eleven pounds and others barely carried four. Some were twins; some were triplets all competing for two teats on one proud, tired ewe. Some came on bright afternoons and others had to shiver in a dark cold midnight barn. But no matter what odds were chalked up against lambs at their births, the shepherd almost always felt content to leave them with their mothers after he had seen them nurse. For milk is their perfect food.

Even as the shepherd folded up his cot and spread clean bedstraw, the nursing lamb was filling out his stomach. His shivering stopped — also his crying — and the world must have looked a vastly better place than when he'd opened his eyes on it. A newborn appears all legs and neck, yet now a fire caught within the lamb's ribs — milk on fire — and its heat toned cold flesh all across his back and fluffed his fleece so that it could trap air and warm him.

It was now past six. Yet the shepherd was not ready to seek his farmhouse and his bed. Not because he feared any longer for this lamb or mother. Not because there was anything more that he could do to help them. But as the devout will sit by icons of Nativity, gazing patiently for hours, so he sat in the still barn and watched until the creeping dawn.

The shepherd had never loved after the fashion of a mother. Men there are who do; as there are women, too, and many, who love in the mode of passion. And there is a third mode of loving, which is husbandry — the care of households — and this love too respects no gender. But none of these three is perfect, every mode of love is fraught with evil even as with good. The ram who loved in passion and had seen the soul once now stood snorting in his pen, alone and bored and not in the least concerned that in his passion of an August morning he had started what had just now been completed. Given the chance, he'd butt his great head against the tiny lamb and lame it, or worse. And the shepherd, who loved in his husbandry and had seen just now the souls of lambs and sheep and men, this same shepherd would put a knife to this lamb's neck — in fourteen weeks, in springtime — bringing the lamb's soul to an untimely death.

Husbandry is a great love, but it is weak and imperfect. And even a mother who loves in her motherhood and sees the soul with each tug at her breast, even mothers in their season do make an excess of loving, giving more of themselves to their young than is quite good for either, as though the joy and satisfaction of motherhood could be prolonged forever. As though the child could never reach adulthood, the lamb never leave his mother's side and run and tup and graze off by himself, all on his own. As though to poison any future love the child might know, setting an impossible standard of self-sacrifice.

The shepherd had felt relieved to see his children leave home. True, it meant a loss of good companionship and help; but he took pride in seeing them go make lives of their own. This was final weaning. The shepherd and his wife had not seen eye to eye on child rearing. She would not have let her offspring stumble; he thought stumbling fine so far as it prevented falling.

She had been a strong and able mother. He had loved her for that; but they had had differences. This is what drew him up short when he would start to build a perfect shrine to her, a shrine of memories: They had loved dearly, but also they had struggled one against the other. Raising yet another infant, they might have consumed their marriage. When her womb had swelled again with child, he had felt betrayed. What she loved was plainly children. What she loved was mothering. She was not content to live without a child in the house.

The shepherd believed: In all love there is a co-mingling of purpose, which is good; and yet what creature has not loved his loving more than whom he loved, and to the loved one's pain and detriment? So the ewe, if she would flee the lonely pain of lambing, would flee the ram's obsessive courtship. So the lamb, if he would save his neck, would flee the loving shepherd. So the infant, if he would grow up, must wean himself from the incomparable pleasures of motherlove.

But not for a while. The shepherd blew on his cold hands and watched:
Even now, contracting to expel red afterbirth, Penelope did not prevent
her lamb from poking at her breast. And when the placenta fell from her
and lay upon the straw, she turned round to eat it with a relish, eating
what had served and nourished the lamb in her for five months. The
shepherd watched, for the nativity was yet untarnished. The warm breast
was the lamb's strength, and it was his strength alone, and it was not in
the least his weakness. Not yet.

The shepherd watched, because though he had never loved after the
fashion of a mother, yet he loved motherhood and he loved to see the
miracle.

In the next three weeks the shepherd's thirty ewes bore fifty lambs. The
shepherd took to living in the barn, attending births and watching that
each lamb got off to a good start. He only lost one — a reckless lamb
who jumped into a water trough and drowned. All the others lived, and
grew, and drank milk at warm breasts.

The ewe cannot digest grass; in her first three stomachs flora digest
grass, and in her fourth stomach the ewe digests flora. But the newborn
lamb has no flora in his stomachs, and his body must have fuel to burn
to fight the winter's cold. No accident, then, that the milk of ewes has
nearly twice the fat of cow's milk. Milk fat is a perfect fuel to burn.

Yet more than keeping warm, the newborn lamb must grow. His body must have perfect protein, and must have it in abundance. No accident, then, that the protein in milk is complete; and the milk of ewes has half again the protein of cow's milk.

Pound for pound, ewes milk like cows. And ewes milk at their own expense. No matter how well the shepherd fed his milking ewes, they lost weight each day for two months. They burned themselves, they gave away their bodies' fine condition. They mined their bones of calcium. They lost all fat. They tired. But their baby lambs grew strong and healthy.

Through the coldest month of winter, which is January, the shepherd let his lambs grow out on milk. On milk alone. His twins grew a half pound every day, and single lambs a whole pound, and this in the teeth of winter. The shepherd fed his lambs by generous feeding of their mothers: two pounds of grain a day to ewes with twins, a pound a day to ewes with single lambs, and all they desired of the green first cut of hay. Thus hay and grain made milk.

When the shepherd's wife had nursed her babies, many years ago, she herself drank nearly two quarts of cow's milk every day. And the woman's milk was good, and sweet, and raised a son and daughters strong and fair and in good health. As humans say, drink milk to make milk. And yet, thought the shepherd, what a grander feat of nature's art when ewes make milk from hay and corn.

Does it feel, the shepherd wondered, like draining one's life away? Into these rambunctious creatures. They'd come dancing in a pack across the yellow bedding straw, each turning aside to find its mother and poke at the breast. Lambs would drop upon their knees and lift their thirsty

Dancing in a pack

mouths and punch the bags impatiently to bring down milk. And each ewe would turn and tickle her baby's bung with her nose, setting its long tail to waggling: for a mother must smell her own lamb before she will give suck.

It had not been like that with the shepherd's wife, nursing her babies. Just hearing the infant's cry could start milk flowing from her nipples. Sometimes mere thoughts triggered those white streams in her breasts. Proofs of love like these awed and disturbed the shepherd; the feelings he bore his children seemed weak in comparison. Perhaps they were not. But yes, it was like draining one's life away. Yet eagerly. Like sacrifice. Like giving up one's life only to find it: like a passing of the torch, like gazing on the living souls within all creatures, though not with the external eye.

Milk is perfect food for lambs. It is also perfect food for all manner of flora that would invade ewe and lamb and cause both grievous suffering. Not because bacteria hate sheep; any more than sheep hate the living grass they bite and chew; any more than the shepherd hates the lamb he'll roast. All living creatures on the earth are fair game to each other in the epic poem of food; and in this is good and evil, for the good and evil in this world are inseparable, and both are quite necessary. Yet in husbandry men erect fences to help certain goods and hinder certain evils.

Although seeing white milk flow from breasts awed and disturbed the shepherd, although he could scarcely imagine how those streams must feel, yet now he spent each day involved with milk, involved with breasts, managing lactation to grow lambs and not dangerous flora. He sought to keep his ewes from making more milk than their lambs desired — only just enough. So he weighed each lamb at birth and tried to guess its appetite, because a ten-pound lamb will be more thirsty than a five-pound lamb, and three six-pound lambs — born triplets — will be very thirsty indeed.

When the shepherd weighed his firstborn lamb, it weighed nine pounds. The shepherd knew his ewe Penelope to be an able milker, and he was concerned not to overload the lamb's stomachs, nor to flood the ewe's breast. Once he'd had a lamb who took his fill of milk from just one teat, and never found the other until it was cold and blue with spoiled milk, which is called mastitis. More than once he'd had lambs die — and barely at one week of age — from overeating milk, a very nearly perfect food but deadly when a newborn gorges himself, drinking more than he can digest, letting harmful tiny creatures run riot with the excess until the intestines bleed and black waste oozes from the bowel.

So the shepherd brought Penelope green hay and warm water, but he declined to give her corn or oats or wheat for some days — and then only sparingly, at first — to keep her milk production balanced with the lamb's best needs. When the lamb grew apace, he would have no difficulty handling all the milk his mother could produce; then the shepherd would increase her grain, and all would be well.

On a sunny afternoon the shepherd held each lamb in turn and quickly cut its tail off, and pressed it close to stop the bleeding. He disliked to do this, but it was part of his husbandry. Lambs get stomach upsets that can paste their woolly tails fast against their bungs, blocking all the passage of their waste into the world. Little lambs can die this way, untimely and in bitter pain. The shepherd found no joy in mutilating his lambs' bodies; yet he did this evil with deliberation, that a greater evil might not come to pass. Then he sent each lamb to find its mother and be loved again and nurse the swollen breast. It saddened him to see each mother turn to sniff her lamb where now no tail waggled, but only a bloody stump. It saddened him to see their tails piled dead upon the floor. Yet he told himself: The souls of lambs do not reside in tails. He had the tails, but the lambs still had their souls. And presently they came to gambol and to play again.

The shepherd had, in former times, altered the bodies of his ram lambs in another way: by gelding them. As the bull become a steer, as the cock become a capon, as the boar become a barrow, so the wethered ram grows docile and eats with more dedication — for it is his only pleasure. Yet the shepherd had discovered wethered rams, for all their size, were adding more fat and less muscle to their growing bodies. Because shorn of their cod, they did not run and play and tup.

Now fat is a good thing, and a wonderful thing in its place; but too much fat in a man's belly will make him grow fat himself, and sluggish, till he makes an end of husbandries. The shepherd preferred to eat the muscle of his animals, in which is better health and strength. And it made him angry to see men trim pounds of white fat from their meat and throw it out as garbage, a waste of feed. Better the animal had not been made that fat. Also, the shepherd enjoyed his lambs and loved them better when they raced around the barn and leaped all four feet in the air and played at tupping as young sheep are wont to do, rather than to see them stand dull-eyed before the manger.

In any case, the shepherd meant to kill his ram lambs before they could truly tup, for the work of passion somehow toughens a ram's meat. He meant to kill them before they might tup their own mothers, too, getting them again in lamb; so he did not fear to leave their testicles intact. After the shepherd had cut the tail from each lamb, he was content to sheathe his knife until another day, and glad to spill no more of his lambs' blood than husbandry demanded.

The lamb drinks milk and grows. A pound a day, the firstborn grew, because his mother loved to nurse him, and because he had no twin competing to share every meal. By the time the last lamb had been born, the first weighed twenty-five pounds and — whether because he had lost his tail or no — the shepherd could no longer catch him running round the barn. The shepherd had never in his life gained weight like that; and

Bouncing on a ewe's broad back

he had been proud enough when his son had gained a pound a month. A pound every day — the thought was so enormous, he had to wonder how the lamb could even walk. Not to mention how it could feel at home within its body as it burgeoned toward maturity.

Yet, surprising the barn on a winter's afternoon and seeing twenty lambs all sleeping on each other in cold sunshine, the shepherd admitted they looked quite at home within their bodies. And at night he'd see them, two or three at once all bouncing on some ewe's broad back where she lay tolerant and bemused and not seriously trying to sleep. Or he'd see twins race across the barn and leap onto their mother, demanding that she wake and stand and give them the warm breast again. From the first week of their lives, the shepherd also saw lambs mount each other in the game of tupping, though they could not truly tup. All around the barn the young would chase, playing their mating games.

Seeing all these things, the shepherd wondered if he'd ever been at home in *his* skin as much as these creatures were. Perhaps not. And perhaps human passion and human motherlove were ghosts or vestiges of stronger feelings when we were more creaturely, somewhere back down the long forced march of our evolution. Yet the shepherd would not have changed places with his lambs. If his nose had lost the scent of passion, if his wife had never sniffed her infants as they suckled — and known who could say what pleasure? — still as humans they possessed a greater means to love and see the souls that dwell in creatures and in humankind. Greater, though less strong. And its name was care: was husbandry.

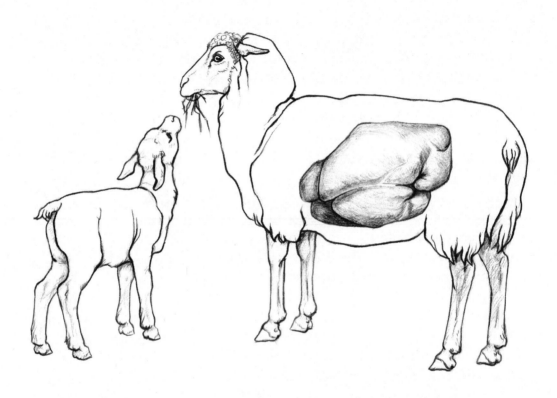

5 ❧ The Lamb Eats Grass and Grows

THERE IS EVIL IN THIS WORLD, AND GOOD, AND BOTH ARE related as the two sides of one coin. So a lamb is guided to a great good which expends much life: He learns to love grass and eat it to grow flesh and fuel his body.

Even by the nightfall of the day that he was born, Penelope's lamb had pulled leaves of grass from her own mouth and tasted June-cut hay. He nibbled thoughtfully, imitating her, though his rumen lacked the flora he would need to make a meal of grass. Yet each day he tried again, and learned to choose the leaves from stems and how each different grass must taste, even grass cut long ago and stored in the dry barn to feed grown sheep in winter.

The firstborn lamb would never harvest his own grass on pasture, never taste the lush intoxicating April clovers, or May dandelions, or the bitter chicory of June; never taste the yellow trefoil in midsummer heat, or the brittle timothy of August. The firstborn lamb was destined for an Easter slaughter, destined to be killed untimely by his own shepherd. The firstborn would never know the pleasures of the pasture which is every sheep's true habitat and a triumph of the art of nature, who is all our mother. And, though the shepherd had learned by seeing souls of lambs not to dwell upon death in his mind, still he was a little sad to think his firstborn lamb would never gambol across the feast of an abundant field.

Each day, even as a baby, the lamb nibbled some few blades of grass, pushing beside his mother at the manger. He could not digest these. They were nonetheless essential to starting the slow machine of rumination. Slow: because a young lamb cannot fill his rumen with a grassy wort and pitch the working yeast as would a master brewer; each lamb must acquire and nurture his flora slowly, daily, bit by bit, colonizing all his first three stomachs. Slow: because the microbes that digest alfalfa are not those that digest brome, and those that break down timothy may have nothing to do with clover. Slow: because green grass, ingested, takes some five days to be processed through a sheep's dark gut.

Milk is perfect fuel for lambs, and easily digested, and is rich in fat which is a concentrated energy. Grass is quite a different thing. The fuel in grass is cellulose, a carbohydrate so complex it binds together some three thousand glucose units. Cellulose is the building block of all the world of plants, strong, yet so flexible that two-foot stems of timothy and hundred-foot oaks can both support their weight and withstand a gale. As men harvest trees to burn wood — cellulose — in coldest winter, heating wooden houses, so sheep burn hay — cellulose — to warm their souls and fuel their bodies. All creaturely life must make heat, and make it by expending other life, and this is food and nourishment and life and death and good and evil.

By the time his firstborn lamb was one month old, and had grown from nine pounds up to thirty-four pounds, and could run and jump and never be caught in the open barnyard, the shepherd saw that he ate hay by the mouthful, eating with a relish and fighting for his own place at the ewes' long manger. And the shepherd saw the dry pelleted dung his lamb produced, like a grown-up sheep's dung now, and no longer the yellow milk-dung of the newborn; and the shepherd knew his lamb could set a proper table now within his paunch to feed the flora he had gently nurtured in their population of his stomachs.

The shepherd was reminded of the tender second-cut hay he had made early in August, to feed lambs in winter. He broke open one such bale, and he took his lamb aside where hungry ewes would not shove past him, and he offered tender second-cut hay to his firstborn lamb. The lamb ate it heartily. The shepherd remembered then the heat of summer, three fine fair hot cloudless days, three in a row, when he worked in blazing sunshine to have hay for this moment.

The shepherd built a creep in one corner of his barn, where sun streamed through a window on bright February afternoons. A creep is a place where lambs can go but ewes cannot, because no ewe can squeeze her shoulders through the narrow entryway. In this creep the shepherd built a manger just the size for lambs, and a lamb-sized salt lick and a lamb-sized water trough. Then he filled the wooden manger with second-cut hay. Lambs

A place all their own

love to explore and to play in a place all their own, so in a few days the shepherd saw his firstborn had much company inside the creep. All the lambs were tasting tender leafy hay and eating it.

We do not speak yet of weaning, which is a complex good and evil, and quite necessary. We speak here of weaning's precondition, which is solid food. For though milk is perfect nourishment for baby lambs and humans, both still crave in time for more than milk. Our mouths grow teeth — and baby lambs are born with teeth — and we would bite the very breast that gives us suck, could we not use them. In fact, the shepherd had filed more than one lamb's sharp incisors with an emery board, to prevent their wounding irreparably a ewe's soft teats. All our bodies long to function as their architecture purposed: whether we have eyes, to see; whether testicles, to tup; whether teeth, to bite and chew and fill our mouths with solid food.

The child, however, rarely weans himself while mothers will give suck; nor will little lambs. The shepherd recalled how his wife had nursed their youngest for three years — well past the time when he was ably chewing meat — and only weaned him because she took sick with flu, and lost her milk. The boy could not give up suckling while his mother loved to nurse. Like these lambs, he had one foot in the world of infants and another in the world of adults, loving the breast and yet familiar with new cravings that no breast can satisfy. Lately all an infant's joy, overnight the breast becomes one happy pastime among many. We do not speak yet of weaning, but of weaning's precondition in the confusion of loving breasts while growing teeth.

The shepherd had his own thoughts about weaning, as a husband of animals must. Some lambs in this world are given but a month to nurse, and others are left on the breast all through a summer's pasture season. Different shepherds husband differently, for different reasons.

The shepherd of the ewe Penelope — and of her lamb — sought to grow the finest spring lamb he could while feeding the least grain. He sought to do this because he believed in grass and in the art of nature in creating animals that are equipped to nourish themselves with grass. Even humans with their one stomach can make a meal of corn or wheat, or oats or rice, or rye or barley. And the soil that best grows these grains is scarce throughout the world: It must be flat and clear and rich and watered regularly. But the world is full of land well suited to the growth of grass, which weaves pale roots all through the earth and forms the warp and woof of sod which holds the soil against rain and wind that would erode it.

The shepherd did not wish to take the corn which might have fed a human, and feed it to his sheep, and place sheep therefore in a competition with humankind for food. He loathed this; yet he saw it as a necessary evil. Ewes heavy in lamb and denied grain may founder with ketosis, or their lambs may be born scrawny and half dead. And grain spurs the gush of fresh lactation; the ewe nurses better, more abundantly, and wastes less of her own flesh. Yet after two months of nursing, ewes produce less milk; increasingly, they use grain to rebuild their own bodies after the rigors of bearing forth and feeding lambs. Still they have long months ahead to regain their former condition; they will not come into heat and long to tup again till August.

So the shepherd urged his lambs to eat the green hay in their creep.

They lived briefly in two worlds, those of milk and solid food. But the shepherd counted the days till he could safely wean them, putting a firm end to milk.

The lamb ate grass and grew. The firstborn never had a name, because the shepherd knew its end would be untimely death, death before fruition, death in springtime; and it would have saddened him to call the doomed by some bright name. Yet the shepherd was not unhappy to watch his lamb grow, and was not ashamed to examine the broad muscling of the lamb's thighs and his shoulders, where there is much good meat. As the shepherd felt along the lamb's bony spine, where lie the rack of rib chops and the loin, he felt no guilt to look upon the creature that he loved as food. When the shepherd saw his firstborn play at tupping other lambs, or gamboling across the snowy barnyard to suckle his mother, or racing to the creep to eat of tender leafy hay, then the shepherd took joy in his labor and his husbandry: Because even a doomed lamb, one marked for untimely death, even such a lamb could live his days out full of joy, knowing all the thousand pleasures of life in a body, which is all the temple of our souls.

6 ❧ The Lamb Eats Grain and Fattens

THE EYES OF MEN AND ANIMALS MOST OFTEN GROW OPAQUE with age and lose the unqualified sparkle that becomes an infant. The shepherd had coveted the innocence and light in young eyes, particularly now that the best his own could muster was a determined ingenuousness — and not even that for long, nor often. But so little evil befalls a well-mothered infant; and it is evil that slowly dims the light in eyes.

To be sure, lambs lose their tails; and many infant rams must endure surgical amendments to nature's art in their manhood. Much like circumcision. But when one is cold, there is the warm mother to nestle with, and when one is hungry, she gives milk — abundant, perfect food; and very largely every need a lamb or child might have is satisfied — to foster growth. And somewhere near a shepherd or a husband putters seeking ways to fence out evil from the infant's life, and to fence in good.

When the shepherd's firstborn lamb was nine weeks old, however, and weighed some sixty pounds, a catastrophe befell him and all the forty-eight other lambs in the barn. Evil — to the shepherd, a complex good and evil, wholly necessary; but to the lambs, an at first unmitigated nightmare. We speak of weaning.

The lamb will never wean itself, nor the child, while its mother willingly gives suck. And yet the grain the shepherd had been feeding to his ewes, to make milk, to grow flesh of lambs — this grain now would grow more flesh if fed to the lambs themselves. Accordingly, each day for one week the shepherd reduced his ewes' grain. They in turn produced less milk, so that a lamb might suck as though to fill his stomach but leave off with barely a wet whistle. The ewes' swollen udders began a slow deflation, until once again their teats would set like buttons on their bellies.

The ewes complained bitterly at losing their sweet grain.

The third day after he had fed his ewes no grain at all, the shepherd penned all his ewes and lambs in close together. Now he walked among them without chasing, holding each in turn. He led each ewe from out of the pen into the open barnyard, leaving lambs behind, and he swung the barn door shut so that the ewes could not re-enter. Although the lambs could not have known it, though they did not say it, yet each lamb bid farewell to the warm breast and to motherlove, which is a very strong love, powerful like passion, though not so great a love perhaps as husbandry, which yet is weaker.

Now the shepherd moved the ewes' long manger out into the barnyard, and he moved their water there. March had broken winter's back. The bitter nights were over.

The lambs did not at first perceive that they had lost their mothers. But their mothers knew, and set to wailing to the shepherd and to their lambs through the barn walls, because they had loved to suckle lambs, and loved to mother them. When the lambs within heard their mothers crying out for them, they cried too; and the din was enough to drive even the shepherd, who loved sheep, from his noisy barn. But before he left, he tore apart the creep he'd built for lambs to eat their tender hay in — because now all the barn was theirs — and he brought out long troughs where he poured grain, just enough for each lamb to fill his mouth one time.

Very many lambs refused even to taste this corn and oats, thinking instead of breasts and of the warm milk that had vanished. But in time the shepherd knew his lambs would come to relish grain, which is sweet to grind between the broad teeth far back in the mouth. Solid food. No more were the lambs torn, living in two worlds.

All night the lambs and ewes cried to each other, and all the next day. On the evening of the second day the shepherd held each ewe in turn and felt her breasts to make certain they were not becoming sick with milk. Milk within the udder must be drained or reabsorbed or it will spoil in mastitis. Then the breast may never milk again, and the shepherd would have had to cull that ewe out of his flock.

Because the shepherd dried his ewes off slowly, though, weaning them from daily grain, he found little to distress him now in feeling each ewe's breasts. One or two — mothers of twins — he milked out. Tasting their rich milk so warm and frothy in the pail, the shepherd wished he could for one day be a lamb and suckle. But he knew this was an idle thought; he had been weaned once, forever, forty-seven years ago; he would never be a lamb; his end was death and he could not reverse for a single day his life's course toward that end. He even guessed it was his heart that would kill him, for it raced some nights out of control as on the day his wife died. He knew he could be no lamb. Yet he did enjoy ewes' milk, and drank his fill from the clean pail. No milk to an adult, though, can mean what it must to infants.

Two days later he checked his ewes again. He found them dry.

As he had decreased his ewes' grain slowly, so now the shepherd gradually accustomed his lambs to eating grain. Each morning, before throwing leafy second-cut hay in their wooden manger, he offered them whole corn and oats and wheat all mixed together. But he never offered more than they would eat. When he saw the first signs of a lamb with scours — diarrhea — he would take that lamb aside and give it no grain for a while. For grain is rich food for lambs, full of energy, but too much grain too soon will make lambs sick and stall their bodies' growth.

The shepherd saw that there were three weeks yet till Easter, when many people feast upon the roasted flesh of lambs. He went to his barn and held each ram lamb to weigh it, and he sought to choose which of his lambs might be made fat in time. He chose six — all born early, all born without twins — who were already of good size. Some of these weighed sixty-five pounds, some weighed seventy. These he marked for slaughter.

Then the shepherd held each ewe lamb, examining their bodies to see whether they were fit to become full-grown ewes and bear their own lambs. One he found — a fair one, too, named Rachel — whose lower jaw he discovered to be overlong and poorly shaped. A sheep has eight teeth across the lower jaw, incisors, which bite grass against the upper gum or pad, which has no teeth. Lambs with teeth which badly miss the pad can eat barn feed and suckle; turned onto pasture, though, they face starvation. The shepherd was sad to see the ewe lamb with her jaw defective. Yet her body was of good size, and might fatten before Easter. Untimely death seemed not so evil as to put the creature onto pasture without a sound mouth to eat grass and prosper.

The shepherd took his six large ram lambs and his ewe lamb with the undershot jaw, and he built a pen for them off in a sunny corner of the barn, apart from all the other lambs. He was glad to see the ewe lamb play with the rams in this pen. He believed that even creatures raised for meat, for human stomachs, even these deserved to live normal lives; and he liked meat better when it came from lambs he knew had run and chased about and played at tupping.

For his forty-two other lambs, the shepherd was content to see them grow more slowly. The ewe lambs had many months to gain wide hips for tupping and for bearing lambs into the world; and the smaller ram lambs could be marketed well into May, when spring lamb is scarce and dear.

The shepherd now built a creep gate in his broad barn door, so that the forty-two lambs could run into the barnyard with their mothers, yet the mothers could not regain the barn and eat the lambs' grain or their tender

Hoping to nurse once again

hay. Some of the lambs found their mothers and cried out for milk. They dropped on their front knees to punch the bag with thirsty lips, hoping to nurse once again; but the bags held no milk, and the lambs rose disappointed. Yet most of the lambs had come to put away all thoughts of milk, and nevermore would place themselves as supplicants before their mothers. They had been weaned: They had known some sorrow, and the taste of grain.

In the Easter pen, the shepherd changed the rations of his seven lambs until each ate equal parts of grain and hay. This is a rich diet for a lamb, full of energy, and their bodies grew nearly a pound each day. The shepherd watched his biggest lamb — his firstborn — eat his grain and fatten, and this fattening pleased him. He had seen meat on some tables swathed in such a bark of fat it fairly outweighed the lean muscle, and the shepherd thought the men who fed those animals had wasted grain. But the shepherd knew his lambs were lean. He could feel their ribs' arc plainly all across their flanks, and he felt each vertebra along their loins. A little fat is a good thing, pleasing to the tongue and stomach, and giving men tremendous energy to burn. So the shepherd did not stint to feed his lambs mixed grain and hay.

The days grew longer. March warmed the earth and broke the back of winter. And the sun moved past its equinox into another spring.

A show of pride, of ego

One April day horns erupted on the firstborn lamb's white head. The shepherd was proud — though they were tiny horns — proud, as when his son's face had grown whiskers. Because in his male sheep, horns were a sign of adolescence. The shepherd supposed his lamb could truly tup now — and give seed — though the ewe lamb in the Easter pen would never come in heat. He was glad he'd left the ram lamb's cod intact, because a wether grows no horns.

The fattening lambs now made a show of pride, of ego, and of the vigor that is passion's precondition. Some husbands of animals hate to see their fattening creatures exercise and butt their heads, seeing only wasted feed when energy that might grow flesh is burned to fuel activity. The shepherd was not one of these. He liked to think his lambs knew all the joys of living creatures, and he preferred to eat a muscled leg he knew had loved to run once, rather than a leg that had stood fixed and sluggish at the feed trough all its fattening days.

On the Wednesday before Easter, the shepherd held each fat lamb and took its ear tag from its ear and weighed it on his scale. He loaded five of the six ram lambs and the little ewe lamb onto a truck, and drove them to the slaughterhouse, and he took the wages of his husbandry from the packer. It troubled him to leave his animals all trembling in a strange place and a house of death. He had preferred to kill them each one with his own hands. But the law forbade him to slaughter except for himself, except for his own table. So he charged the packer to slaughter his lambs quickly, because they were unhappy and afraid to be in his dark house; then he returned home again.

The shepherd's firstborn lamb had yet three days to live, and the shepherd fretted to see him penned up all alone. So he tore the pen apart and let the firstborn run outside with all the flock and see his mother again, though the firstborn sought no mothering.

The shepherd left his firstborn in the barnyard. He had dull knives to sharpen in the love of husbandry.

7 &❧ The Death of the Lamb

ON A BRILLIANT APRIL MORN, THE SHEPHERD PUT HIMSELF in mind to kill his firstborn lamb. There is evil in this world, and good, and both are necessary, and both are as two sides of one coin. To kill a lamb or any creature — to kill anything — is to do it a great evil; yet food is a great good to our bodies, where our living souls dwell. Nourishment is good, but nourishment demands that men do evil, whether plucking fruit or pulling roots out of the earth, whether threshing yellow grain or putting the knife to a lamb. All these evils ought to be done with a right mind.

Yet there is a special mind, an equanimity for slaughter. Because — whether plants have souls or not — the souls of living creatures that run and tup and suckle young are very like our human souls. And in his husbandry, which is one mode of loving, the shepherd had often seen the souls of lambs. He dreaded to do them evil; yet he would eat meat, and it seemed more just to kill meat for his own table than to have another do it. And kinder to his firstborn lamb, who trusted him and would not fear. It seemed appropriate to finish, insofar as his own stomach was concerned, the long cycle of husbandry.

The shepherd oiled a whetstone and sat in his kitchen, sharpening a caping blade with slow, circling wrist strokes. The knife could not be sharp enough. It seemed to him an honest tool, fitting for the evil he had set himself to do.

The shepherd had seen many sheep taste death, and by no means all at his hands. He had seen much evil done to creatures at their lives' dispatching; some evil done in the name of humane slaughter, some evil done in the name of thorough bleeding, some evil done in the name of safety and convenience for the men whose work it is to kill. Fads and fashions come and go in slaughtering, as in all things. Lately though the shepherd considered that what made slaughter "humane" did not involve technique, or tools; not questions like whether to stun with ax or sledge or pistol; whether to hang before stunning; whether to stick before hanging; whether to hobble or to let a stuck creature run bleeding till it dropped upon the earth; whether to shoot from a distance or with the gun pressed next the skull — these were phantom issues. The real issues were: Is the creature going to its death in fear and terror? And is its pain in dying made worse by man's cruelty?

To the shepherd, slaughterhouses were a necessary evil. The finest technology cannot quench the fear a simple creature knows at being trapped in a strange place. The shepherd had seen fear in the eyes of his six lambs, penned at the abattoir with frightened cows and calves and pigs, waiting for a door to open that no creature walked back through.

It was little consolation that the killing was efficient — was practically painless. The terror, that was inhumane.

The pain of death is something different. The shepherd had tried to understand pain, and particularly pain in dying. It was because he guessed his wife had died in horrid pain. Unspeakable pain. She must have. Yet her face, in death, showed no emotion. That astonished him. No more agony than if she'd pricked a finger, sewing; no suggestion of the massive hemorrhage in her torn womb. How could her face show no pain?

The shepherd had seen sheep face a hundred pains — some fatal, most not. The pain of bloat and hoofrot and ketosis. The pain of limping bloodied where wild dogs had torn flesh open. The blue pain of mastitis. Pain of weaning, pain of heat, the charged pain of August tupping. The convulsive pain of lambing. The shepherd had watched sheep endure pain, and endure pain bravely, as creatures with souls: because the soul informs us that much pain is necessary evil, necessary and inextricable from the good in this world. Pain is one price creatures pay for consciousness, whereby we feel our lives, and love, and see the souls within each other. So the soul informs us not to seek an end to every pain; yet we would end certain pains, as shepherds try to fence in certain goods and fence out certain evils.

Selfishly or otherwise, the shepherd sought to keep his sheep from many kinds of pain; but he considered that in certain painful matters anaesthesia was greater cruelty than pain itself — in that anaesthesia would cheat a creature from the knowledge of its life. One such painful matter was the slow event of birth. And another such matter was the quick event of slaughter. Painful, and yet, rising out of pain, one feels the living soul.

The shepherd chose not to end the life of the lamb he loved with a quick concussion, with an unseen blow from nowhere, with a gun exploding at the skull. He had seen the souls of lambs. He believed the soul knows how to die, even as it taught us once to endure birth's grip, and to love the good and hate the evil that are in this world. Of evils, he believed the least was killing simply with his knife: watching with the creature some quick seconds while blood spurted from its neck, bringing on unconsciousness as in a swoon, a tidal drift, but not as an explosion. He could do this while speaking to his lamb and gentling it, and watching with it — watching it go headlong into death as it had entered life. There was no terror for the lamb, and the lamb's death was not cruel, and the shepherd himself could not wish for any better death; though he could not plan his death, as who can? Yet he never wished to be deprived of it, as in concussion.

He thought: Only let the blade be sharp unto perfection, for then it slices flesh as though flesh were butter. He had accidentally cut himself, one day, with this same knife — and had seen the meat within his body. The blade had been very sharp; what he remembered was not pain.

And he thought: There is another thing. A gun, a blow is easy. But to bring death to another creature, one that has a soul, that should be no easy matter.

The shepherd sought a special mind, an equanimity for slaughter, because slaughtering his firstborn lamb would place him briefly at the center of the epic of good and evil that is food, which is life, which is death; and he expected to be awed and overwhelmed, as always when he slaughtered.

Down the years, the shepherd's thoughts had changed about this equanimity, about the right mind for slaughter. For too long he'd tried to justify himself — as though he could. He'd said to himself: This is a creature I have raised for slaughter, raised it from the moment of its birth. Never once did I think of permitting this creature to become other than meat, meat of a lamb killed untimely, killed before fruition. I have purposed this with all my skill at husbandry; nothing could more justify my slaughtering the lamb.

However in the fact of death the shepherd saw the soul depart the lamb, and seeing this he no longer felt justified.

Again the shepherd thought to justify himself, as though he could, as though justification were a proper mind for slaughter. He thought: I left my warm bed for a cold barn to see this lamb aborning, squeezed trembling from a trembling ewe. And in the cold I waited there to see that all was well, to see the mother lick it clean, to see it stand on spindly legs and wobble toward the swollen breast. And had the lamb been fearful to enter the wide world headlong, had he turned his face as though to stare back at the womb's collapsing, then would I have entered the ewe's womb to turn the lamb aright, feeling all birth's dark contracting heat; and then my arm, withdrawn, would have shivered soaked with birthing fluids even as a newborn lamb, yet with no ewe to lick me dry. And in my husbandry I've saved the lives of lambs — of many lambs — and saved their souls to live more days within their growing bodies. I have saved lambs; nothing could more justify my slaughtering one.

However in the fact of death the shepherd saw the soul depart the lamb, and seeing this he no longer felt justified.

Or again the shepherd thought to justify himself, as though he could, as though justification were a right mind for slaughter. He thought: In August heat I sweated in the sun some three fine fair hot cloudless days, to make the tender hay I knew lambs would love to eat. I bought the land on which I made that hay; I worked to make it fertile; I seeded down the grasses that I knew a lamb would relish. I bought the tractor, and the rake, the mower and the baler; I put a new roof on the barn to keep my stored hay dry. I built all the fences round the pastures where the brood ewes grazed from Easter until heavy snowfall, where they came in heat which is the fire to nurse a lamb in winter, where they did conceive and grow lambs in their dark expanding wombs; and my fences let them graze and tup and grow their lambs in safety, safe from dangers they had never contemplated. And there are one hundred unseen fences I've erected for them, fencing out some of the evil and fencing in some of the good in this world, for that is husbandry. My work and my husbandry are all the reason that these lambs exist, and nothing could more justify me now in taking one for slaughter.

However in the fact of death the shepherd saw the soul depart the lamb, and seeing this he no longer felt justified.

One last time the shepherd thought to justify himself, as though he could, as though justification were a proper mind for slaughter. He thought: I am a shepherd, a man who loves sheep after the mode of husbandry. And love is a great good because in love we see the souls in fellow creatures — and our own souls — and yet love is a great evil for no love is perfect. A ram loves after the mode of passion, hot and strong, consuming. Without this love no lamb had ever been conceived. Yet the ram's love is all olfaction, passing short, soon forgotten. Given the chance, the ram would wound his own get grievously, butting heads until the lamb's head ran red blood, until the lamb would fall and not regain his feet. Passion is a necessary love and a strong love, but its real object is not ewe or lamb. Its object is itself. Passion is no perfect love. And again a ewe loves in the mode of motherhood, a very strong love which endures much pain and would gladly sacrifice life itself that the lamb might live. Perhaps there is no stronger love. And yet I think the mother ewe would never wean her lamb — as though to cripple the young and make a wound of mothering. Have I not seen ninety-pound lambs nursing on eighty-five-pound mothers, their flesh wasted in lactation? Love that will not wean cannot be perfect love, it cannot have at heart the lamb's best interests; love that will not wean is perfect love of mothering, but not perfect love of lambs. And in my own love as a shepherd, as a husband of these creatures, how should my love for the lamb be more perfect than ewe's or ram's? I loved the lamb; but more, I loved my husbandry — as the ewe loved mothering, as the ram did love to tup. We none of us have loved perfectly. Yet none of us loved badly. We loved each as best we could, given what creatures we were. And so I am quite justified in slaughtering the lamb, because no love is perfect. Slaughter is but my love's imperfection.

However in the fact of death the shepherd saw the soul depart the lamb, and seeing this he no longer felt justified.

The shepherd whetted his steel blade with circling strokes, deliberately, thinking of all the ways he'd tried in former times to justify the slaughter of a lamb. As though he could be justified, as though justification were a right mind in which to slaughter. Since his wife's death, though —

since the day the soul departed her — he had abandoned justifying good or evil. He only sought to live with eyes open, with deliberation. The shepherd found the equanimity he sought, and he was ready.

He walked to the barn and fed green first-cut hay to all his ewes, and tender, leafy second-cut hay to all his lambs. While the firstborn lamb was thus distracted at the manger, the shepherd wrapped arms round him and held him on the floor and bound three of his legs together with baling twine, hobbling him. He spoke to his lamb, gentling him, and the lamb was not afraid because he knew his shepherd.

Then the shepherd carried his lamb into the familiar barnyard, apart from the ewes all at their manger. He laid the lamb upon the table that he had prepared, three clean boards set on sawhorses. He held the lamb upon its side, pinning its shoulder with one knee, and then he stretched the neck and slid his knife in just below the ear. The blade was very sharp, and sliced flesh easily, and the shepherd knew the lamb had scarcely felt its neck cut open. He spoke to his lamb, gentling him, as the blade found the veins and arteries that serve the brain. He severed these; and the lamb's heart pumped a gush of blood — blood from all the lamb's living flesh, a cup running over — into a pail the shepherd held. His bowels moved, as they did once in birth's painful grip; and the lamb's pizzle grew hard as though intent on tupping.

The shepherd spoke to his lamb, gentling him, and the lamb was not afraid though he perceived his life was ending. With the thick neck muscles severed and the lamb dizzied from lost blood, the shepherd snapped the lamb's neck back across his knee, and broke it. After that the lamb lay still. And the shepherd said: I never can be justified in doing

Killed with equanimity

this, for there is no justification. Yet I do this as one who must eat, as one who relishes the taste of meat. And as one who is himself meat, and will feed worms in good season.

The shepherd killed the lamb with equanimity — with grace — thankful that for one more time he was the eater, and not yet the food.

The lamb never shut his eyes, yet as the shepherd watched he saw the soul depart the lamb. And he thought: I believe and I see that the soul exists, and that it teaches us to love the good and hate the evil that are in this world, and yet to accept them both, for both are necessary. And without a soul no creature could endure its birth or dying; and without a soul none of us could endure to fill his stomach — no, not once — because the good and evil in all food would surely drive us mad, had we not our souls to help us comprehend the mystery.

8 ❧ *The Dissection of the Lamb*

THE LAMB LAY DEAD. THERE WAS, HOWEVER, MUCH LIFE left within the lamb. There were tissues in the lamb that would not taste of death for hours, and there were some cells that might live on for days inside the carcass, like remote platoons in war who miss the news of final truce.

Truce? Death is not a truce. Alive, an animal fights constant battle with infection; but when the soul departs, its body quits resistance. New life took up in the slaughtered flesh immediately. So the shepherd went about his work with all deliberate speed. Only his hand stood between the muscled flesh and rot.

He had another, more pressing reason to work quickly: all the flora in the lamb's dark paunch had certainly not heard of death, and would not cease their patient work digesting grass, and multiplying, and creating gas. But the gas had no escape now. Once the soul departs the lamb, eructation ceases. The fat stomachs bloat alarmingly. They must be liberated from the carcass before they would literally explode.

The shepherd knew that at slaughterhouses animals are held off feed a full day — sometimes longer — before they can taste death: just to clear the stomachs, to minimize this risk of bloating. The shepherd, too, had once imposed this fast upon the lambs he slaughtered. It had been the only day in all their lives they were not fed, and their cries would fill the air — cries very like fear. Sheep are creatures of utter routine, slaves to routine, and the fundamental routine of their lives is eating. Out on pasture, ewes spend half the hours in a day just grazing. And eight hours more lying still, chewing grassy cuds. No privation could be harder on a lamb than going hungry.

The shepherd had learned to spare the lambs he slaughtered from this death fast. But he paid a price: He had to dress them with the utmost speed to free their burgeoning stomachs. So, blood on his hands — and his heart racing, moved again by death, and on the verge of letting go his equanimity of slaughter — now the shepherd grasped one of the lamb's front knees and whittled off a swatch of woolly pelt. As every time before, the white flesh underneath surprised him: that it should be so clean — sterile, in fact, till that moment. He sliced a line up through the pelt from knee to near where the lamb's heart hid inside the brisket. He repeated this cut on the other foreleg, cutting as it were a wedge from knees to heart. Then he matched this front wedge with another at the rear, running through the pelt from hind hocks to the bung.

Now a brood ewe quit the manger and came to inspect the shepherd's business. She was not the dead lamb's mother, not the ewe Penelope.

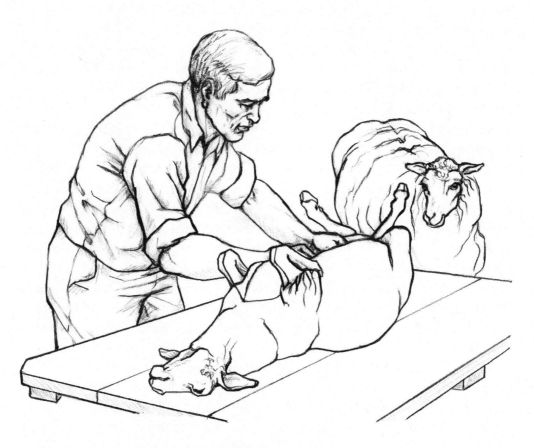

One brood ewe inspects the shepherd's business

The shepherd thought to make a fuss, to wave the ewe off, lest she nose the dead and dwell on slaughter in her mind. But she stared from some few paces, and it seemed she could not recognize the dead as any sort of creature, least of all a sheep. She turned and walked away. The soul had departed the lamb — though little else had changed. Oh, there was a bucket of spilled blood. But the shepherd looking in the bucket did not see the lamb's soul.

With clean hands he stood astride the lamb and pushed his fingers under the wedge of skin he'd cut from knees to brisket. Inside, all was warm — lamb's heat, warmer than our human bodies by some few degrees — the warmth held in by wool. Making fists to probe and tease, he worked the flesh up off the carcass. Bit by bit, his arms crawled in up to his elbows. His heart raced. Then he walked round to the dead lamb's rear and fisted from the bung up toward the head. At length, the woolly pelt that swathed the lamb lay loosened from its belly.

The shepherd's arms grew tired, and his heart, and he wished to pause to gather spirit. For it is a fearful thing to push arms underneath a creature's skin, even a dead creature. Especially a dead creature. And it is a fearful thing to strip a creature of its hide. But because the lamb's stomachs had begun to swell, because the shepherd had not starved it, now he took no rest. Knife in hand, he teased the tendons in the hind legs free from muscle, and he laced them through with baling twine. Then he climbed upon the table where the dead lamb lay, and pulled with all his strength to hang the lamb suspended from a tall white ash — the tree itself all swollen with red buds to set out spring-green leaves to shade the barn in coming summer. With his knife, the shepherd sliced down the midline of the belly from the bung to brisket.

Now the shepherd teased the pelt from the lamb's hind legs, and cut around the bung, and peeled pelt from flanks and back. The flesh inside was pleasing: firm muscled legs and sirloin papered evenly with fat. Next he fisted pelt from carcass from the foreleg to the brisket; the muscled shoulders pleased him too. There was much good meat here. Finally he freed the pelt all down the lamb's spine, tail to neck, and the pelt hung inside out shrouding the head of the dead creature.

The shepherd's spirits calmed, for the lamb no longer looked as if it had run and played and eaten hay not half an hour before. But its dark paunch swelled against the breast. Slitting the lamb's neck lengthwise, the shepherd teased the windpipe that serves lungs with air from the white-ribbed gullet. He tied the gullet shut with twine. Now no food could leave the stomachs as he pulled them free.

Yet the stomachs are one with the coiled intestines, and the bowel; all these must come out together. Accordingly the shepherd cut around the lamb's bung, circumscribing it till he could pull six inches of bowel from out of the carcass. With more twine he tied the bowel shut, sealing in pelleted dung.

Now the lamb's digestive tract — thirty pounds within the ninety-pound lamb — was as a corked flask of wine still fermenting, bound to burst. Quickly the shepherd opened the warm carcass at the cod, cutting open the lamb's breast halfway to the heart. The stomachs puffed out against the opening, and the shepherd had to reach inside and hold them back gingerly with his fingers, lest he puncture one and taint his meat with vapors of digestion.

Finishing this cut, the shepherd raised a bucket to receive the digestive tract. He hauled it out: the bowel, the snaking white intestines, the garnet liver with its green gall bladder sac, and the four stomachs. Now and then he reached inside to sever a fleshly attachment; but the guts of sheep and men alike are very largely tunnels unto themselves, one dark road from mouth to bung, and points of contact with the sterile bodies that they serve are few, and easily detached. There is in sheep a white excelsior to pack the stomachs — caul fat, which the shepherd liked to melt upon a roasted leg of lamb. He peeled this fat free and set it on a tray for edibles. Then he cut the three leaves of the liver free, excising the gall bladder and the bile duct — for fresh lamb's liver is delicious, but bile imparts a bitter taste to any meat it touches. The shepherd cut the gullet free below where he had tied it, and withdrew that from the carcass.

The lamb was now completely gutted.

The shepherd carried his bucket of stomachs some distance from the carcass, and downwind, and punctured the dark paunch to let stored gas escape. So again he saw the hay he'd fed his lamb for breakfast, already being digested by flora unaware they were without a host that would have digested them in good time. New bacteria were already preparing to digest the thick stomach wall, and they would die in turn. Yet something would remain — some rotted waste to nourish the soil, to help summer grasses grow and flower.

The shepherd returned to the carcass of the firstborn lamb. He could work more slowly now. The bomb of stomachs had been defused. He cut the bean-shaped kidneys from the lower back, and the firm kidney fat, and he placed these with the edibles. Then he cut the tongue out of the head, and teased the thymus gland, or sweetbreads, from the open neck.

With a saw, he next cut the head off altogether, skinned it from the pelt and dropped it in the pail of stomachs. He was quite calm now. He thought he should be more distressed — it was in the head, if anywhere, he felt the soul should live: the head which bears the eyes, and ears, and all the mysteries of olfaction, and the brain in which the lamb had held the trust he'd borne his shepherd even while the shepherd killed him. Yet examining this head the shepherd was certain that the lamb's soul had departed it, leaving something useless and inedible to humans, fit to feed dogs or to bury in his pasture. But the pelt he draped across the barnyard fence to cool. He would make something warm of that to wear in winter.

Finally the diaphragm remained, a tough membrane. Cutting this he tore out lungs and heart. Because he disliked lungs, he threw them with the offal. But the heart he set with edibles. His own heart, he thought, was not much bigger. Smaller than his fist. And tough — tougher than any other muscle in the body. Remarkable, that when he brushed against mortality the pace of this red pump should quicken. But it was impossible to mistake this heart for soul.

Now the shepherd lowered the lamb's carcass from the budded ash, and sawed off the hind hoofs at the pastern; these he threw away. Then he grasped the fetlock joints upon the lamb's foreshanks, and with his knife he broke them clean in two. To a butcher this defines lamb: The fetlock joints must break. Had the lamb lived some more months, the cartilage

Suspended from the budded ash

of the joint would have calcified, or turned to bone, and then no knife could break it clean, and that is mutton to a butcher.

So the shepherd had these things: the lamb's dressed carcass, and its pelt hanging upon the fence, and a tray of edibles, and a bucket of red blood and stomachs and inedibles. He carried the carcass and the edibles into his house, and laid the carcass on the kitchen counter. Taking salt out of his cupboard, he went back into the barnyard to salt the fresh hide. He hung it on a high beam in his barn, to cool and to let the salt wick out its moisture.

The shepherd took a shovel and went out into the tupping pasture, where he dug a hole to bury the lamb's offal and head and hoofs and blood. Doing this, he noticed that green grass had started growing again. It was springtime. Nothing now hindered him from turning his sheep out to graze some hours every day and taste the lush grass of early spring.

When the burial was finished, and the sod set back in place, the shepherd returned to his kitchen to cut up the carcass. With knife and saw he cut off each hind leg, which is the thigh and sirloin. Each leg weighed six pounds — or nearly what the lamb himself had weighed when he was born. The shepherd was well pleased. Then he cut the flank and breast off either side, to bone and roll as roasts. He cut the foreshanks off, to braise and boil down in stews. He cut the shoulders off by sawing in between the fifth and sixth ribs, and breaking the back. He thought: It is all too easy. Even strong backs break with ease. And he broke it once again to separate the rack from loin. So easily might he break his own

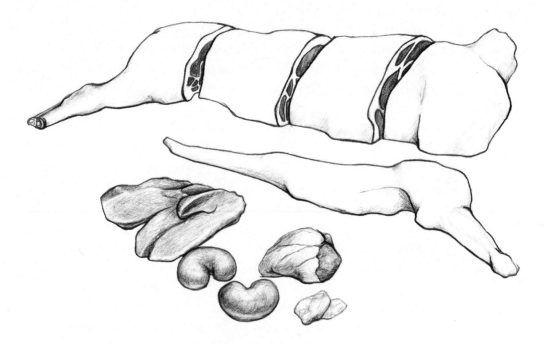

Fresh-killed meat

back, in a simple fall. The wonder was he'd lived so long. The wonder was, he'd lived.

The shepherd boned each shoulder, leaving pockets in the meat to stuff to make fine roasts. He knew that cells inside these bones might well be still alive, not having yet heard of death. But when he examined them and tasted their pale marrow, he knew they did not contain the lamb's soul. So he weighed the shoulders, boned, and each one weighed four pounds. The shepherd was well pleased. He cut the neck up into chops by sawing through vertebrae. All that now remained was to cut apart the rack and loin.

The shepherd was suddenly hungry. He had killed the lamb at nine o'clock; now it was almost noon. Though in slaughter's equanimity he did not wish to eat, nor in taking off the pelt, nor in burying the offal, yet now the fever of his emotions had subsided. So he melted butter in a frying pan upon his stove, and sliced one of the leaves of liver, and sliced the bean-shaped kidneys. He fried these while he cut the loin and rack up into chops.

Then the shepherd sat down at his table to eat fresh-killed meat.

9 ❧ The Souls of Lambs

THERE IS EVIL IN THIS WORLD, AND GOOD, AND BOTH ARE necessary, and both are as two sides of one coin. The shepherd looked at what lay speared upon his fork, and what had lain alive not three hours ago within the creature that he loved. Organ meat: liver to feed blood, that blood might feed the cells all through the body of the lamb; and kidneys to clean blood of waste, to flush the body clean. Here was meat, simply; and yet to the shepherd meat was never simply meat. Meat was vocation, and love. Meat was an obsession, strong as instinct, strong as instinct bursting into love in passion and in motherhood.

He put the meat into his mouth, and chewed, and tasted, which is perhaps as close as humans come to the rich maddening world of creaturely olfaction. The shepherd thought: Meat — this taste of fresh-killed meat — this may be to me what sniffing ewes in heat is to a ram, what licking afterbirth is to a ewe, and nosing a lamb's bung to tease it while it sucks the teat. And the shepherd relished his meat — more than he could say, more than he could have remembered — for of tastes and scents the memories of men are passing short.

The shepherd thought: I loved the lamb. I loved watching its passionate conception — in a moment, in a ewe all fevered in the tupping pasture — already nearly nine months ago. I loved to feed the ewe that she might feed the fetal lamb growing heavy in her womb. I loved to attend the lamb's birth — already three and one-half months ago — and to see it stand and find the breast upon a bitter night. I loved to see the lamb grow, I loved to feed it hay I made in August heat, and grain to put a bloom upon its carcass, fat feathered through muscle.

Yet I killed the lamb. For all my love of it was husbandry, a mode of vision to see the souls that dwell in creatures; a mode of vision much like passion, much like motherlove, and yet greater in a way, and yet also less strong. Greater, because husbandry is *chosen* love. This is human. Rams cannot choose *not* to tup; so their loving is not chosen. And what person, too, has not felt driven by instinctive passions? Likewise, ewes cannot choose *not* to love their lambs; so their loving is not chosen. And human motherlove feels equally instinctual. But to *resolve* to care for others, to love based not upon instinct but upon intention, to intend to care for others in deliberate patterns — that is husbandry. And that is very nearly all that makes humans more than sheep. And brotherhood is husbandry, and love of friends is husbandry, and love of children, too, and much of the love between men and women is all husbandry. And husbandry is why we live in houses, rather than on pastures, and why we build cities, build societies and governments and nations and strive for one world —

for an ever larger household. Husbandry is what has made us human, made us more than creatures.

Yet the shepherd thought: I killed the lamb. For husbandry, although a greater mode of loving, is yet less strong than instinct. Husbandry would temper passion to create a state of marriage. Husbandry would temper motherlove to wean the little child — first from milk and, later on, from motherhood itself. Husbandry would never kill the little lamb to make a feast, no matter how delicious. The shepherd thought: Husbandry, the care of households, that is much of what is best in humans. Yet humans are creatures, too, and never can be otherwise while they live and carry souls. There is evil in this world, and good, and both are necessary. I was hungry and I craved fresh meat — craved instinctively — and instinct is a stronger force than all resolve to husbandry. So I killed the lamb, for I was human but a creature too. So the mother, for all she may try to temper motherhood with husbandry, to free her child, still she either makes a wound of mothering, crippling her young, or else the child rises up and rebukes her for her motherlove. And many men there are who love in this same maternal mode.

The shepherd thought: I killed the lamb. I loved it as a husband but I could not let go instinct; I hungered for meat. So the man who loves in passion, for all that he tries to temper passion with good husbandry, to make a marriage, to make of love a way of daily life, much more than raw olfactions, much more than instinctual attractions — yet though husbandry is a greater love than passion, passion has the strength of instinct. And women there are, and many, who love in the mode of passion. Good and evil in this world are as two sides of one coin; we cannot have it otherwise. The shepherd thought: I loved the lamb, I loved it as a husband, I cared for it and I saw its soul through husbandry, and yet I killed it. For my body craved its meat.

The shepherd now was sad, and all his plate of meat was empty. To cheer himself, he tried to minimize what he had lost. He counted what it took to grow this lamb — that had dressed forty-four pounds of meat — to see how little of the earth's resources he had squandered. He thought: I have used the life of one ewe for nearly a year. And that had cost one fifth of an acre's growth of pasture grasses, and one tenth of an acre's growth of meadow grasses for the hay to feed her through the winter. And the grain I fed her, that had cost the use of one year's growth on one sixtieth of an acre someplace where fields wave with grain, to make her strong at lambing time and fill her breasts with milk. And the lamb's own hay, the tender second-cut of August, that had cost one twentieth of an acre's growth of grass. And the lamb had eaten nearly as much grain as its mother.

All together, the shepherd considered he had used the growth of one third of an acre of land upon the earth for one year, to grow the lamb and to keep the ewe that mothered him. One third of an acre, and nine tenths of that in grass which holds the soil and never needs be torn up with the plow. He thought of a field such as men play sports upon — such fields were roughly one third of an acre in size. But this saddened him, because a playing field can seem a very large place; yet he wanted to believe he had not squandered much of earth's resources to produce the lamb he killed. Then he thought of prairies, and vast sprawling ranges, and high pastures on broad-shouldered mountains, and of all the fertile land on earth, billions upon billions of acres that can grow green grass. He imagined flying high over the earth, looking down on grass spreading everywhere to the horizon. Then a playing field did not seem so large to raise a lamb, and to feed the lamb's mother for a whole year. The mother, too, would be meat one day, he reminded himself. And then he was sad again, because he would have loathed to eat Penelope.

The shepherd rose and cleared his plate. He wrapped his meat for freezing, so that he could eat the lamb's flesh over several months, and not in one great feast as many do at Easter. The shepherd's stomach was well satisfied, but in his mind he was agitated and unhappy. He had killed the lamb, for meat, and now the lamb's soul had departed and it was not buried in the pasture, nor packed in his freezer, nor draped with the pelt across a high beam in the barn. He could grow another lamb: another year, another one third of an acre: small quantities of time and land. Yet the soul he loved, that particular lamb's soul that he killed with his own hands — that soul he could never see again. And throughout the world, men were marking spring's rebirth by eating lamb, the life that came in winter. The shepherd asked himself: Will husbandries forever be betrayed by instinct's appetites? Is this the end of all our caring?

The shepherd's stomach was now satisfied, but his mind was not at ease. And he thought what he fought not to think: When his wife had died, that too had been a failure of his husbandry. He had valued hay — he'd valued sheep — more than the woman he loved, that dark afternoon. He had been nearsighted, and confused. Even could he not have saved her — probably he could not — he might at least have watched some moments with her while her soul departed. He might have seen that, and shared it. He had loved her deeply; but husbandry has deep weaknesses.

Now the shepherd felt his pulse race.

Yet a miracle occurred: The lamb's flesh — his body, broken, in which the shepherd was certain he had seen no soul — the lamb's flesh was now incorporated into the shepherd's own body. And his stomach churned, performing miracles, and he thought: Truly, men become what they behold. We are what we eat. Though I cannot understand this.

His heart found its ancient pace.

He knew that he had not eaten the lamb's soul. Yet eating, and incorporating, he remembered the lamb and all the hundred times he'd seen the lamb's soul through his husbandry, which is but a very great and yet a weak mode of loving vision, all having to do with fences, all having to do with cool intention, with patterns of deliberate caring. And as often as he ate of the lamb's flesh, he knew he would remember. And when he had eaten all, yet somehow the soul of that lamb would reside within his soul: would dwell in the house of his lord forever. Likewise he felt his wife's soul now. He had not truly lost her; no, he never could. He never hoped to understand this. But he knew it must be true.

So the shepherd's heart grew glad again. He felt the lamb inside him. He thought: Eating flesh we nourish flesh, and yet we can do more. We can love and see the souls that dwell within us once again. Eating — taking nourishment — that is resurrection.

Nourished, now the shepherd's body coursed with energy. He thought: It is afternoon, and grass is growing in my pastures. I should walk the fences and check gates and stiles, and if all is well I'll turn the flock out

Tightening frost hove fences

to taste spring grass. He pulled his boots on, and so doing he thought: We are creaturely *and* human; our instinctive appetites must always war with husbandries, and yet, and yet lust for passion, motherhood and even meat lust, these lustings make all husbandries possible. Without these lusts we would be nothing, we would not exist.

Nourished in his belly, the shepherd saw the two sides of one coin. It seemed to him a miracle. And in his tupping pasture he beheld another, stooping near the firstborn's grave to tighten fences where they sagged, frost hove: Grass can nourish flesh, but yet again dead flesh can nourish grass. Now the shepherd wept, though not in sadness. But he realized that at his table, eating meat, he had forgotten to say grace. So he said it now: For the good and evil in this world, thanks. For nourishment, thanks. And for husbandries — for husbandries, particularly — thanks.